LINLITHGOW

LINLITHGOW
SIX HUNDRED YEARS
A ROYAL BURGH

William F. Hendrie

JOHN DONALD PUBLISHERS LTD
EDINBURGH

ISBN 0 85976 271 8

By the same author
Discovering West Lothian (John Donald Publishers Ltd.)

Phototypesetting by Pioneer Associates, Perthshire
Printed in Great Britain by Bell & Bain Ltd., Glasgow.

Foreword
by The Right Hon. Tam Dalyell, M.P.

Bill Hendrie has given us a 'bean-feast' of a book — a treasure-house of fascinating information.

He describes Christmas at Linlithgow. A mixture of worship and festivities with the first celebration on St Nicholas Eve. The reader can conjure up the choir boys from the Song School in the Kirk Gate visiting the Palace to sing carols to the Kings of Scots; then, being entertained to an unusual supper. The highlight was the production of an enormous Christmas pudding, or dumpling. In it, was one solitary bean. Each chorister received a slice, and the lad who was lucky enough to find the bean was given a special present by the Queen. Bill Hendrie says that it was from this simple amusement that we get the term 'bean-feast'.

Bill Hendrie's knowledge of local custom from the culinary to the chivalrous is encyclopaedic. As a teacher and headmaster he has communicated his enthusiasm for local history to hundreds of pupils. As a Member of Parliament, whose service spans the period of Bill Hendrie's career in West Lothian, I am in a position to know about the dynamic influence that he has had on his pupils, and about his capacity to illuminate their surroundings for young people. I also know of the gratitude that many of my constituents, now in their discriminating 30s and 40s feel towards Bill Hendrie. Any reader who begins this book will be gripped by his writing, and discover why he is so well-loved in the West Lothian Community.

In this 600th Year, in which we are honoured by the visit of Queen Elizabeth, all of us who care about Linlithgow owe Bill Hendrie our thanks for his Labour of Love, making our past come alive.

Tam Dalyell

Acknowledgements

I have received a great deal of help in the preparation of this book from many of the people of Linlithgow. In particular I offer my thanks to Councillor Jimmy McGinley, representative on West Lothian District Council for Preston Ward, Tom McGowran, Secretary of the Linlithgow Festival Committee, Dave Roy, Secretary of Linlithgow Rose Football Club, who provided all of the information about the club, Jimmy Dumbreck, who likewise supplied all of the details about the West Lothian County Cricket Association, Barbara Braithwaite, Colin Galloway, Bobby Thomson and Ian Ballantyne. My thanks also to Jean Brady of West Lothian District Library for her patience as always during my researches at library headquarters at Wellpark, Bathgate. Finally, my thanks to the Royal Commission on the Ancient and Historical Monuments of Scotland for permission to reproduce the illustrations on pages 18, 44, 46, 59, 60, 64, 72, 97, 99, 103, 125 and 142.

This book is dedicated to all of my pupils, past and present at Linlithgow Primary School. I hope that I have taught them to take a pride in their town.

Contents

CHAPTER ONE

Dreamthorp

'DREAMTHORP — a castle, a chapel, a lake, a straggling strip of grey houses, with a blue film of smoke over all, lies embosomed in emerald.'

'Nothing could be more peaceful. The hands on the clock seem always pointing to one hour. Time has fallen asleep in the afternoon sunshine. I make a frame of my fingers and look at my picture. On the walls of the next Academy Exhibition will hang nothing half so beautiful!'

So wrote Victorian author Alexander Smith, whose best-known essay, 'Dreamthorp', gave Linlithgow its well-known nickname.

Today the mist of blue smoke has disappeared from over the palace, the kirk and the loch, for 'Dreamthorp' has long since stirred and wakened from its 'Brigadoon'-like slumber, but despite modern developments, Linlithgow remains as beautiful as Alexander Smith painted it a century ago.

Besides the beauty of its natural setting and the fascination of its regal history as far-famed birthplace of Mary Queen of Scots, Linlithgow owes much of its awakening to its excellent situation almost midway across Central Scotland between Edinburgh and Glasgow and on the main railway line and the M9 motorway. These swift and reliable means of transport have persuaded thousands of new families to choose Linlithgow as their home and have turned it into one of Scotland's fastest-growing towns, boosting its population from 3000 after the Second World War in 1945 to over 12,000 in 1989 as it proudly prepares to celebrate the six hundredth anniversary of the granting of its royal charter.

There can indeed be few Scottish towns in which the past plays a more prominent part in present everyday life than Linlithgow, with everything from parking to holidays influenced by its history. Fortunately, the 'Folk who live on the hill', as the newcomers from the spreading, sprawling housing estates of Deanburn, Priory, Oatlands Park, Laverock Park, Beechwood and Riccarton are often known, and their even newer neighbours from the even more sprawling Springfield, are on the whole as possessive and protective of Linlithgow's past as the true 'Black Bitches', as the original natives from Lowport to 'Lithgow Brig still almost defiantly 'cry' themselves. For having found their 'Dreamthorp' tucked away in the valley between the Erngath Hills to the north and the rolling green Bathgate Hills to the south, they are determined to cling to and cosset the customs which make their town distinctively different, from its town crier to its 'Peelie', the special policeman who patrols its royal park and from its traditional annual Riding of the Marches to its post of Provost, which it alone among all Scottish small towns persists in retaining despite the local government re-organisation and the regionalisation of 1975, events Linlithgow has never forgiven.

To Linlithgow, of course, little more than a decade of footering with local government is nothing compared with its past, which it can trace way back beyond the days of recorded history, right back to geological times, which shaped the physical aspects of the town.

Essayist Alexander Smith wrote that he always thought of his little 'Dreamthorp' Linlithgow as a warm, summer place, 'with its daisies running up to every cottage door, a passing sunbeam making brilliant a white gable-end and a whole troop of swallows skimming about the great tower of its ruined castle rising high in the rosy air', but at one time this spot must have been unbelievably, bitterly, freezingly cold.

For as the thick sheet of ice spread south-east from the Highlands during the Scottish Ice Age, it entirely ensheathed where Linlithgow now lies, scraping away the soft layers of sedimentary rocks, forming the valley and leaving behind the ice striations on the neighbouring hills, which can be seen particularly clearly to the east on the steep slopes of Binny Crag, which the glaciation carved into a crag and tail formation similar to those topped by Edinburgh and Stirling Castles.

It was upon its retreat as temperatures slowly rose again, however, that the band of ice had its greatest effect upon the spot where Linlithgow was to grow, because as the ice melted it discarded its terminal moraine to form the drumlins or little mounds, such as Baronshill, which are a feature of the eastern approach to the town. Even more important, it soon afterwards cracked and dropped an enormous chunk of ice. Gradually in time as the land re-emerged from its icy embalming, this gigantic ice cube slowly melted to form Linlithgow Loch. And from this feature it is said Linlithgow took its name, meaning the stretch of water in the damp double hollow.

On the spit or nose of land, which sticks out into the loch and gives the effect of that double hollow, was to arise Linlithgow's most famous building, the royal palace of the Stewarts, but long before that the loch itself was to be the site of the town's very earliest dwellings.

For it is believed that they grew up as a crannog, a cluster of homes on stilts built out in the loch, whose waters gave protection to Linlithgow's earliest inhabitants in Scotland's dangerous prehistoric times. Tradition has it that the crannog from which Linlithgow traces its origins was situated close to the south shore of the loch in what is now known as Town Bay and that these homes on stilts were given added protection by being reached by a submerged causeway, whose abrupt twists and turns were known only to the local inhabitants.

While all traces of the crannog have long since been washed away, there is ample evidence of other occupations of the Celtic tribes in the surrounding area. Just as ease of defence dictated the choice of the waters of the loch for the crannog, so again defence appears to have influenced these early inhabitants to pick high ground for their settlements ranging from a cromlech close to where Kipps Castle was later built near the slopes of Cockleroi, to hill forts at Ochlitree, Bowden and Carriber. The first part of the name Carriber is in fact probably derived from the Celtic word for fort as at Carriden near Bo'ness, where the Romans started their outermost line of defence, Antonine's Wall.

Although there are no Roman remains within the bounds of Linlithgow, it is known that the main road built by the Romans to connect their port at Cramond with their harbour at Blackness, midway between Carriden and Bo'ness, passed just to the north of the town and that the well on its route from which Walton Farm takes its name was originally sunk by them to refresh their thirsty legionaries before they tackled the final climb over the crest of the Erngath Hills.

While Erngath is now the accepted spelling for the five hundred foot high ridge of hills which separate Linlithgow from the River Forth to the north, in the past they were often spelt Airngath or Irongath, and this name is said to come from the fact that many swords, spears and other weapons were recovered from their slopes following a great battle fought some say between the Romans and the Picts and others simply between rival local tribesmen. This legendary local battle also gives rise to the other well-known local placename of Swordiemains on the steep Flints Road between Linlithgow and Bo'ness, as many swords were later ploughed up in the fields belonging to the farm occupying this site.

Another connection between the days of the Roman occupation of these parts and Linlithgow caused considerable excitement in 1781, when a farmer ploughing on another local farm, Burghmuir, near where the new electronics factory is situated at Springfield to the east of the town on the road to the M9 motorway, turned up a pottery urn full of Roman coins. The find is described as follows in the Second Statistical Account of Scotland, the chapter on Linlithgow being written in 1843 by the minister at St. Michael's, the Rev. Andrew Bell. According to him the Roman coins, 'had been deposited in an earthen urn, which the plough broke, and were picked up in lumps, by some persons who followed it to gather stones. The town as superior claimed the treasure. The pieces were not above the size of a sixpence, all silver, and having different dates and impressions. They were probably the collection of some virtuoso, and being involved in rust, would furnish a sweet morsel to antiquaries. Some coins were also found lately in an old house in the town, when the workmen were digging for sand, about 500 in number of which twenty were gold, the rest silver. Many of them had impressions of the different James's, and some were Henry IV of England. These had their lustre unimpaired but the silver pieces were overgrown with rust.'

CHAPTER TWO

From Hunting Lodge to Royal Palace

WHILE Linlithgow was born of the Ice Age, it was as Alexander Smith's summer place that it first attracted Scotland's kings. For it was as the site of a hunting lodge, where the monarchs and their courtiers could spend the night, that Linlithgow first gained its regal status.

King David I, who reigned from 1124 to 1153, like many of the nobles of his time loved the thrill of the chase, but after the fall from his horse which led him to found Holyrood Abbey in thanksgiving for his survival, it is said that he became reluctant to make the often dangerous ride back to Edinburgh after dark. Thus, rather than curtail his enjoyment of the hunt, it is claimed that he gave orders for the erection of a royal hunting lodge at Linlithgow around which in the rolling Bathgate Hills, near Torphichen and down over Bathgate Moss, some of the best sport in Scotland could be enjoyed. Linlithgow was also a convenient resting place between Edinburgh and Stirling Castles.

The promontory of land jutting out into Linlithgow Loch offered an excellent site for the new royal dwelling because, as well as the magnificent views afforded by its hilltop situation, the waters of the loch on three sides formed a natural moat, thus making it easily defensible, just in case any rival nobles thought of attack when the king, having lingered long and late hunting the deer and wild boar, chose to spend the night there.

The hunting lodge, upon whose site Linlithgow Palace was eventually to arise, was, to begin with, most likely a very simple structure. Built of wood, it consisted probably of a great hall with a hole in the roof for the smoke to escape from the open central fire around which the king and his followers could cluster to heat themselves, while animal furs and deer skins on the floor and on the walls would have given added warmth.

Although he enjoyed the pleasures of the hunt, David was also a very religious man. As well as founding Holyrood Abbey in Edinburgh, his very liberal donations of properties in his burghs and domains to the monasteries led one of his successors on the Scottish throne to pay him the somewhat grudging compliment that 'he was a sair saint for the crown', and in Linlithgow this generosity took several forms. These included the granting of a house in the town to the Abbot of Dunfermline, and the gift of all hides from his Lordship of Linlithgow to the monks of Holyrood, but most important of all was his decision in 1139 to place the kirk of St. Michael's and all of its lands both within and outwith the burgh into the hands of the Bishop of St. Andrews.

One of the earliest written mentions of Linlithgow thus comes in the records of the church at St. Andrews where it is stated in the register for the years 1162 to 1172 that the chapel of the Knights of St. John of Torphichen is bound to pay one silver mark annually to St. Michael's as a substitute for burial dues.

As well as their Scottish headquarters which they had at this time recently established in Torphichen, the Knights also owned lands in Linlithgow itself and are credited with running one of the earliest hospitals in Scotland at St. Magdalene's to the east of the town. Traditionally the Knights were always famed for their treatment of lepers St. Magdalene's sometimes being known as the Lazar House while the hill behind is still called Pilgrims Hill. Whether or not these unfortunate patients suffered from as severe a form of this terrible skin trouble as the disease which still exists in some tropical parts of Africa and Asia is not known, but there is no doubt that in medieval Scotland the fear of it was great and is reflected, for example, in the leper squint the remains of which can still be seen in the south-west gable wall of St. Michael's.

For while the Knights like all good churchmen of the Middle Ages were insistent that all of their patients must take part in worship, the other members of the congregation were far from keen to come into contact with the lepers. The solution, both at the Knights' headquarters at Torphichen Preceptory, named after the Christian precepts which the Knights always promised to obey, and at St. Michael's in Linlithgow, was the skilful construction of leper squints, special windows built on a slant or squint through which the lepers could in turn see or take a squint from outside at all that was going on at the altar during the saying of Mass, without distracting the other worshippers with the sight of their terrible deformities.

As well as the now blocked-up leper squint at St. Michael's in whose space the crystal communion vessels are displayed behind the font, Linlithgow's other famous leper squint can still be seen in the Chapel Royal at the palace. Whether or not anyone suffering from a contagious disease such as leprosy would ever have been allowed within the walls of the royal palace may seem questionable, but no less a personage than King Robert the Bruce did believe that he suffered from this plague. On the other hand the so-called leper squint high on the north wall of the palace Chapel Royal may not be a leper squint at all. Its slanting construction may have been for another reason, to provide defence for the Scottish kings when they were at their most vulnerable when kneeling in prayer, and it may therefore have been a guard window from which the monarch could be protected against any assassination attempt.

Another suggestion is that if the strangely shaped window in the palace Chapel Royal was indeed a guard window rather than a leper squint, then what it was designed to guard may have been somewhat more prosaic than the king's life. For as in the case of a guard window in St. Mary's Church at nearby Queensferry, it may have been built to dissuade any little palace servants from being tempted to sneak in to steal the communion wine.

In the Middle Ages it appears that it was not just the morals of the palace servants which might be questioned but those of the religious, the monks and the priests themselves, because another traditional tale in Linlithgow maintains that the clergy at St. Michael's often found it hard to keep their vows of celibacy and that instead of using the covered cloisters in the church's clerestory strictly for prayer and contemplation, they frequently delighted in using these high covered walks as convenient places to meet the nuns from the town's convent at nearby Manuel on the shores of the River Avon.

Manuel, near where the Bo'ness branch railway line left the Glasgow to Edinburgh main line just to the west of Linlithgow, took its name from the Convent of Emmanuel for Bernardine or Cistertian nuns, founded by King David's successor, King Malcolm IV, in 1156. The convent continued to enjoy royal patronage and King Alexander II later gave the nuns the income from Linlithgow's burgh mills, but its site at Manuel Haugh was ill advised and it was always liable to flooding by the river. After the Reformation in the sixteenth century, the buildings were allowed to crumble and in the end the Avon when in spate carried all away apart from one ivy-covered gable wall, which survived to the beginning of this century.

Another Linlithgow religious institution of the medieval period of which little trace now remains was the Carmelite Friary founded in 1290 and dedicated to the Virgin Mary. This was the Carmelite Order's third establishment in Scotland and, like the convent at Manuel, flourished until the Reformation. Today the only reminder of it is the well-known local place name Friars' Brae, but it is hoped that archaeological digs in the grounds surrounding 'Nether Parkley' will reveal more of its past.

It is known that it was situated in what are now the grounds of Nether Parkley, whose previous owner at the turn of the century Mr. J. Henderson succeeded in tracing the walls associated with the north and east ranges of the Friary in 1900. The first professional archaeological dig at this important site took place in 1953, when Miss D. Hunter carried out limited excavations which provided more detailed evidence proving that substantial archaeological remains survived in several parts of the gardens. These were subsequently revealed during major digs in 1983 and 1984 which showed that the first stone built building on the site was over twenty metres in length and over eight metres in width and faced to the east as early churches always did. Although there was no indication of the original use of the building which had once stood at Nether Parkley the discovery of a graveyard in close proximity is taken as an indication that this was probably the Friary chapel. Coins found on the site indicate that it was in use during the late thirteenth and fourteenth centuries. Later this first chapel was extended to form the Friary Church which stretched further to the east and was over thirty six metres long. The added chancel which had walls one metre thick measured almost sixteen metres in length and was eight metres broad. A semi-circular stone built external feature lay against the north east corner of the chancel and was probably the base for a stair possibly leading up to the Friars' dormitory. In addition to serving the needs of the Carmelite Fathers who stayed at the Friary, however, the sheer size of the church may indicate that it was also a place of worship for the people of Linlithgow and the number of burials which took place both within the church and in its neighbouring graveyard seem to indicate that many of them were buried there. Another reason for the size of the church may have been rivalry with the neighbouring Carmelite foundation, St. Mary's, which grew into a substantial monastery on the shores of the Forth at Queensferry where its stone roofed chapel its garth or lawn and the outline of the cloisters which once surrounded it can still be seen.

At Nether Parkley too the archaeological dig revealed evidence of cloisters and also of the chapter house from which the Friar would have administered the day to day life of the establishment. It was situated in the east range of buildings and has been identified as the chapter house because of its better finish than the other rooms which have been unearthed. It had a wooden planked floor and many of the nails used in its construction have been found. In addition the large number of coins found in this area suggest that this room may also have served as the Friary's treasury.

The most southerly room and the largest excavated in the range had a large and imposing fireplace and has been identified as the parlour, the hub of the Friary's social life, where the Carmelite Fathers could gather, warm their hands and talk before sitting down to enjoy their communal meals from which scraps of food debris were found during the dig. Another small room which may have been the kitchen for this frater or refectory was also uncovered as was the well from which the Friars drew their water supply. Equally interesting was the discovery of the Friars' latrine situated to the west of the domestic buildings and indicating their early appreciation of the need for hygiene.

In total over five hundred artefacts, excluding window-leading and iron nails, were recovered during the combined 1983 and 1984 digs according to the excavation leader W. J. Lindsay's report. The most noteworthy included fifty pins and brooches, a decorated finger ring and shards of pottery many from as far away as Saintonge and Beauvais.

It is believed that the Carmelite Friary remained relatively intact for some time after the Reformation, perhaps until 1560, with parts of the south and east ranges continuing in use. Soon after this the ranges were systematically demolished and robbed of building materials until, 'the place of the Carmelite Friars' was ultimately sold for six shillings and eight pence in 1624. Today only local place names including Friars' Brae, Priory, Preston Road and Preston Farm, the Priests' Road and Farm, remain to remind us of this interesting part of the town's past.

It is somewhat ironic that whilst the stones and mortar of Linlithgow's past have disappeared, written records, which at the time must have seemed so much more perishable, have survived, and from them we can learn that the important families in the history of the town in the Middle Ages were the Livingstons, the Dundases, Alexander of Ochiltree and Lindsay of Binny, the latter a name which was to play a very prominent part in the history of the town.

The twelfth and thirteenth centuries were a time of comparative stability, but all that was to change with the sudden death of King

Alexander III, when his horse stumbled on the cliffs at Pettycur and he was thrown as he rode through the night to be with his young French wife at nearby Kinghorn on the Fife coast.

His death could not have come at a more opportune moment for the English. Up until this time the Norman dynasty had been too occupied putting its own house in order and subduing the Welsh, but now Edward I had recently completed the conquest of Wales and had the time and the inclination to turn his attention north. Thus when Alexander's heir, his infant grand-daughter, the Little Maid of Norway, died without ever completing the voyage from Scandinavia, Edward lost no time in interfering in the Scottish succession and was already on his way to becoming the hated Hammer of the Scots.

Resistance was organised by Sir William Wallace, but at the end of June 1298 Edward's army arrived in force. Edward waited patiently to the east of Linlithgow, near Kirkliston, for sufficient supplies to arrive by sea and then by mid-July was ready for the coming fight which took place on 22 July. The night before the battle he spent encamped only a mile to the east of Linlithgow on the Burghmuir. He set up his headquarters in the field to the north of the Blackness Road, which it is said in those days commanded a clear view west as far as Wallacestone, above Polmont, which takes its name of course from the viewpoint from which the great Scottish patriot is said to have looked out to catch a glimpse of the advancing English army.

As darkness fell at last on that warm July night, King Edward settled down to sleep in his tent but, restless as he thought about the fray which the morning must bring, he soon moved outside to sleep beneath the stars. Unfortunately for him it seems that his great battle charger was equally restless because in the early hours of the morning it broke free from its tether and trod on its royal master's chest.

Edward suffered several broken ribs but as dawn broke insisted, despite his pre-battle injury, that his troops move forward through Linlithgow and on across the Avon towards Polmont. His injury proved not to be a bad omen, for at the fray, or the Battle of Falkirk as it became known, unlike the earlier Battle of Stirling his men routed the Scots and Wallace was forced to flee.

Wallace's flight gave the Linlithgow area two links with him. One is Wallace's Bed on top of Cockleroi and the other Wallace's Cave on the banks of the River Avon just upriver from the point where the bridge carries the Falkirk to Bathgate road across the Avon Gorge, in both of which places he is alleged to have hidden after the battle.

If it is true that Wallace was so close to Linlithgow after his defeat at Falkirk, it must have been particularly galling for Edward that his foe slipped through his grasp, for he too stayed in the district seeking treatment for his injured ribs from the Knights of St. John at Torphichen, as they were of course considered to be the best medics of their time. Even more ironic was the fact that Edward sought aid at Torphichen, because it was there at the Knights' Perceptory that before the battle Wallace held his last Scottish parliament.

Edward seems to have been satisfied with the treatment he received from the Knights, because in the years to come he maintained many contacts with them, especially during his long stay at Linlithgow during his campaign of 1301. Winter came early that year and Edward stayed at Linlithgow for three months from 1st November until 31st January, thus giving the town the first of many royal Christmases.

Edward must have been pleased with Linlithgow as a winter head-quarters because next autumn in 1302 he returned and transformed the old hunting lodge into the castle, which Scotland's Chaucer, the poet Barbour, described as 'a Pele, mekill and stark', meaning that this English stronghold was impressively large and strong. The word 'pele' is however a reminder that it was still mainly a wooden structure, for 'pele' is the French word for a palisade of wooden stakes, similar to that erected around the city of Dublin, which gave rise to the saying 'beyond the pale', meaning to be uncivilised or unacceptable.

Unaccustomed to this French word, the local folk of Linlithgow first associated it with the hill above the loch on which Edward's castle dominated the town and later extended its meaning to encompass all the lands of the royal park as it does today.

Just as the saying 'beyond the pale' means unacceptable, so the townsfolk of Linlithgow found the behaviour of Edward because while he built no stone fortifications of his own, employing no masons but only 107 carpenters and 80 ditchers, he commandeered St. Michael's Church and irreligiously incorporated its stone walls into his defences.

Edward had equally little respect for the inside of the church which was utilised as his military storehouse and granary. One cargo, which the Sheriff of Linlithgow was ordered to transport from Blackness and 'store in the Great Church', consisted of '200 quarters of wheat, 60 casks of wine, 300 quarters of malt, 60 quarters of beans, 400 quarters of oats, 30 quarters of salt and 200 quarters of sea coal, the Sheriff finding carriage when he can, at the King's cost, but without hindrance to the works at Linlithgow'.

This desecration of St. Michael's apparently continued at least until 1305 because in that year Edward received a petition from the Prior and Canons of St. Andrews. This stated that, 'seeing he has made a camp and fortalice of their old church within the Peel of Linlithgow, that he would build to them at his own expense a new church'.

In the same petition the Prior and Canons also requested Edward to give them the Chapel of St. Ninian at the West Port and the lands belonging to it and make it a parish church. Edward promised that their requests would be considered by his next parliament, but with more pressing matters such as the increase in strength of Robert the Bruce and his own failing health, they do not seem to have been dealt with. Thus St. Michael's remained one of Scotland's few examples of ecclesiastical military architecture and its castellated battlements overlook the town to this day. It is interesting to note that the church battlements are only on the south, that is the town side of St. Michael's, as presumably attack was only thought possible from this direction.

That attack was likely, however, is stressed by another petition received by Edward in the same year. This came from the Knights of St. John at Torphichen stating that although they recognised that Scotland 'was now settled', they wished to request that those of them who were English be admitted to the Peel at Linlithgow 'for their safety', which seems to question their belief in the English settlement. Soon afterwards the whole position was made even more uncertain by Edward's death and his succession by his son Edward II. Edward tried like his father to hammer the Scots and placed Linlithgow under the command of a French knight, Pier Luband, but the tide was turning in Scotland's favour.

Edward himself occupied Linlithgow during the autumn of 1310 as he tried to counter the ever more effective resistance organised now by Wallace's successor, Robert the Bruce. As the Bruce succeeded in taking more and more of Scotland under his control, the people of Linlithgow were obviously encouraged to fight back, because in the high summer of the year 1313 one of the most famous plots in Scottish history was carefully laid.

The hero was a Linlithgow farmer, William Binny, described by poet Barbour as 'stout carle and a stour, and of himself dour and hardy'. For several years past he had been forced by the English to deliver his crop of hay to the garrison at the castle and knew that he had become a familiar enough figure for security to have become lax.

Farmer Binny therefore arranged on his next trip to the Peel to deliver to the English more than they bargained for. And so beneath the hay piled high on his cart he hid eight Scottish soldiers. As the English sentries in the castle turrets saw the heavily laden hay cart approach as usual from the east, the drawbridge was lowered and the portcullis raised to let it enter.

As always, Binny urged his horse on, but as it reached the far end of the drawbridge he suddenly reined it to a halt with the high sides of the cart and the big load of hay right below the line of the portcullis. 'Call all', 'Call all', he shouted, and at this pre-arranged signal the Scottish soldiers leapt from beneath the hay.

Taken completely by surprise, the English tried desperately to raise the drawbridge but the weight of the cart kept it down, then to lower the portcullis but the wooden sides of the cart kept it up, and, finally, they tried to pull the horse forward, but Binny slashed the trappings and let it bolt into the inner courtyard.

By this time more Linlithgow folk, who had hidden in the bushes around the Peel, had rushed over the drawbridge, under the portcullis and into the castle, where those English soldiers still alive quickly surrendered.

News of the success of this Scottish Trojan Horse soon reached the Bruce, who is said to have rewarded Binny with grants of land, and to this day there are still prosperous farms near Linlithgow called Easter and Wester Binny and many families in the area proud to claim descent from the famous farmer.

For the Bruce at the time, however, the freeing of the castle at Linlithgow proved something of an embarrassment because he did not have sufficient troops to guarantee that he could hold it. Rather than risk the chance of it falling again into English hands, he was forced therefore to order that it should be 'done down'.

How much of the castle forerunner of Linlithgow Palace was in fact destroyed is not clear, but it seems probable that the townsfolk led by Binny, having risked their lives to capture it, were reluctant to see it rased to the ground and only demolished the fortifications added to strengthen it by Edward II's father.

Tradition has it that one part of the castle which Binny and his followers took particular pleasure in smashing was the fortified gateway erected by Edward I, and to this day the massive stone crowned head said to depict the English king himself can still be seen in the palace museum bearing the marks where the Scots took the hammer to 'The Hammer' whom they had so long hated.

Shortly after the English were routed by Farmer Binny's daring surprise attack at Linlithgow, Edinburgh Castle was also retaken by the Scots, and there, in a dungeon, was discovered the former governor of Linlithgow, Pier Luband. Whether he had been imprisoned as a punishment for having lost Linlithgow or for falling out of favour with his English masters for some other reason is not known, but once freed by the Scots he promptly changed sides and later at Bannockburn fought on the side of the Bruce.

His defeat at Bannockburn and the resultant surrender of Stirling Castle to the triumphant Scots left Edward II with no choice but to flee, and as he rode through Linlithgow with the remnants of his cavalry he had no time to stop as he was hotly pursued by the Earl Douglas.

Edward escaped and never returned north of the border but Scotland was not yet free from interference by England and during the childhood of Bruce's heir the little David II, when Edward III seized the opportunity to put his puppet Edward Balliol on the throne, Linlithgow was again annexed.

Denuded of its former fortifications, however, Linlithgow no longer seems to have been seen as a stronghold, the only deed relating to the town and signed by Edward III referring to the church to which he appointed John de Swanlund as priest, in 1335.

By then St. Michael's was already well established as it had been consecrated almost a century before in 1242, when David de Bernham, Bishop of St. Andrews, came specially to the town on 22nd May to perform the ceremony, as part of which he sprinkled holy water, and on each of the twelve spots representing the twelve stations of the cross where it splashed masons later carved twelve consecration marks.

A careful search of the old church reveals that all of the consecration crosses can still be found, but not always where they were originally carved, because during subsequent renovations some of the stones were moved, so that it is now a matter of looking high and low for them. To complicate this historic treasure hunt still further, there are now more than the original twelve consecration marks. The reason for this is that until the extensive refurbishment of St. Michael's this century several of the original crosses were feared lost and some substitute crosses were therefore carved in the apse during the installation of the beautiful oak choir stalls in 1956. To everyone's surprise, however, the recent cleaning and redecoration of the plaster ceiling revealed the originals, together with two hitherto unknown angels, who now look down in fine attire over the nave.

While evidence in stone remains, few written records of either St. Michael's or the adjacent castle survive with the exception of one dated 1350 in which the by then adult King David II granted John Cairns, an inhabitant of the town, the life rent of the peel on condition that he made some repairs to the castle in preparation for his majesty's forthcoming visit to Linlithgow.

Fifteen years later on a subsequent visit to Linlithgow, the King paid Cairns 11s 7½d for safely transporting the royal wardrobe from Edinburgh Castle and £13 6s 8d for arranging a good and plentiful supply of wine for the banquets given during the royal residence.

When he was not busy looking after his royal master, Cairns devoted much of his time to the town affairs of Linlithgow. He was one of the town's two Bailiffs and each year from 1369 to 1379, with the exception of 1373, travelled to Edinburgh as one of the Custumars of Linlithgow responsible for presenting the town's dues at the Court of the Exchequer. Why he did not ride to the city in 1373 is not known, but in that year he sent Thomas a Carson to deputise for him.

In 1376 Cairns was appointed Armiger to the then Earl of Carrick, who later became King Robert III, and from that year until 1379 he worked at Edinburgh Castle, supervising the erection of a fortified tower. The tower cost £302. 12. 8 to build, and in 1379 Cairns was paid an additional £13. 6. 8 for ensuring its completion.

Cairns continued as Master of Works at Linlithgow Palace until 1406, when he was succeeded by Angus de Camera. It was de Camera who introduced the famous eel ark on the loch. This wooden construction was used to keep the eels captive and ensure a good supply of tender young elvers to be smoked for the palace feasts. The multi-pronged barbed iron leinster used to spear the wriggling elvers can still be seen on display in the palace museum, along with several of the original wine bottles, which no doubt provided plenty of good claret with which to wash them down.

This medieval good life well befitted Linlithgow for the town had emerged well from the early Middle Ages. During this period Linlithgow had seen itself established as a member of the Scottish Court of the Four Burghs, Lanark and itself replacing Roxburgh and Berwick on Tweed, which were much too close to the English Border for comfort. Thus Linlithgow was rated along with Edinburgh, Stirling and Lanark as one of the four most important places in the whole of Scotland. It is interesting to note that the original Court of the Four Burghs to which the town belonged subsequently became the Convention of Royal Burghs, which upon regionalisation in 1975 gave birth to COSLA, the Convention of Scottish Local Authorities.

CHAPTER THREE

The Royal Burgh

THE coming of the Stewarts to the Scottish throne brings increasing evidence of their links with Linlithgow and their love for it.

First of the Stewarts, Robert II, was in fact elected and proclaimed king at Linlithgow by the Scottish nobles, who upon the death of David II gathered there and after due deliberation determined that, as the grandson of the Bruce, he was the just and legal heir to the throne.

Robert was the son of Princess Marjory and her husband, Walter the Lord High Steward of nearby Bathgate Castle, and it was from his title that the Scottish royal family, which he founded, derived its famous name of Stewart.

King Robert's right to the throne did not go unchallenged because Sir William Douglas declared that his family had a more powerful claim and intimated his intention to dispute it by force of arms. Fortunately, however, when he heard that the Earl of Moray, the Earl of March and Sir Robert Erskine were all mustering their men and marching towards Linlithgow to support the new king, Douglas wisely decided to negotiate instead and, having obtained the agreement that the king's daughter would be promised to his son in marriage and the post of Justiciar of the whole of Scotland south of the River Forth awarded to himself, he allowed Robert to succeed peacefully to the throne.

During the next twenty years of his reign, Robert stayed at Linlithgow on six occasions and many of his charters were dated from the town.

Most important of these visits for Linlithgow itself was his second last because it was then, 600 years ago, on 23rd October 1389, that King Robert conferred upon the town the status of a Royal Burgh.

The royal charter, translated into English from the original Latin,

Palace, church and Town House form one of Scotland's finest clusters of medieval buildings as seen clearly in this aeriel view of Linlithgow. It was from this heart around the historic Cross Well that the High Street grew vein like to stretch Linlithgow long and lean along the shores of the Loch east to Lowport and in the opposite direction to West Port. In the foreground can be seen the controversial modern Vennel flats while to the north of the Loch stretches the equally controversial M9 Motorway, which many townsfolk feel should have been constructed in a concealed cutting further up the slopes of the Bonnytoun Hills instead of being allowed to intrude into such a historic setting.

reads, 'Robert, by the grace of God, King of Scots, to all worthy men of his whole land clerics and laymen, wisheth health: Know ye that we have granted and at ferme demitted to our lovite and faithful burgesses and community of our Burgh of Lynlithcu, our Burgh aforesaid, together with the haven of Blaknes, the fermes of the Burgh, and petty customs and toll dues, with courts and the issues of courts, and other just pertinents whatsoever: To be holden and had to our said Burgesses and community aforesaid, and their successors, for ever, with all their pertinents above mentioned, in fees and heritage, as is above expressed: paying therefor to us and our heirs, the said burgesses and community and their successors, into our royal exchequer, five pounds sterlings every year and at the usual terms; Witnesses, the venerable fathers on Christ, Walter, Bishop of St. Andrews, and John, Bishop of Dunkeld our Chancellor; John, Earl of Carric, Steward of Scotland, our firstborn; Robert, Earl of Fyfe and Menteith our beloved son; George, Earl of March, our kinsman; Archibald of Douglas and Thomas of Erskyne, our beloved kinsmen, Knights; at Lithcu, the twenty-third day of October and of our reign the eighteenth year'.

The creation of Linlithgow as a Royal Burgh was very important for the town as it meant that from then on the people, without the interference of the king, had the right to choose their own magistrates, or bailies as they were called in the Scottish manner. They were also occasionally known as provosts, but Linlithgow did not appoint a Provost as such until the beginning of the sixteenth century.

In the meantime Linlithgow continued to enjoy its royal connections. King Robert II's last visit came in 1390, shortly before his death. His successor, Robert III, also appears to have enjoyed his visits to the town and there are several mentions in the records of his ordering repairs to be carried out to the royal manor house into which the original fortified castle appears to have been transformed.

One of these for the year 1399 reads that Robert approved the payment of 'forty three shillings for the lead for the building of the king's house at Linlithgow', while in 1405 the same Exchequer Rolls contain mention of another payment of 'five pounds towards the fabric of the manor of the king at Linlithgow'.

In connection with this mention of the fabric of the King's Manor it is interesting to note that in 1397 King Robert wrote to his English counterpart asking him to free a Scottish merchant ship loaded with wood, which belonged 'to the burgh of Linlithgow, lately captured by the English at Whitby'. Wood does indeed appear still to have been the main building material, so·that what with this and the fact that the roofs of the houses were of thatch, Linlithgow must have blazed easily when the English set it alight in 1411. At the same time it must have been comparatively easy to rebuild, just as it had been after the earlier English attack of 1337.

Evidence for this view comes from the customs records for the various Scottish burghs for the period, which show that Linlithgow's trade recovered quickly and that by the close of the fourteenth century the burgh ranked third in the whole country, coming only behind Edinburgh and Aberdeen.

Much of Linlithgow's prosperity was to result from its possession of the port of Blackness, three miles distant on the shores of the River Forth between Queensferry and Bo'ness, the latter of which did not even exist at this period. Blackness was one of the safest harbours on the Forth and Linlithgow's export and import trade carried on through it was surpassed only by that of Edinburgh through its outport of Leith.

Even at this early period much of Linlithgow's prosperity came from the export of hides and fleeces. Higher-quality English wool also appears to have been imported for the town's growing cloth industry.

Linlithgow's trade was, however, interrupted yet again when the English invaded and burnt it for the last time in 1424. This time too the royal manor house was engulfed in the blaze, as was St. Michael's Kirk, thus clearing the way for their rebuilding as we see them now on their shared hilltop site above the loch.

No time was wasted in repairing the ravages inflicted by the marauding English, and rebuilding work on both buildings began the following year in 1425. John of Waltoun was appointed Master of Works for the building of the palace, and this time the enormous sum of £2440 was spent between then and 1430 on constructing it in stone.

Building in stone was however much slower than building in wood, and no matter how hard the masons laboured under master Waltoun, much still remained to be done even after King Robert was succeeded by the first of the James's.

Waltoun too was succeeded by other Masters of Work including Robert Wedale, Robert Livingston, John Holmes and John Weir. At the same time work proceeded apace on St. Michael's and it was sufficiently restored to allow Queen Joanne, wife of James I, to worship there in 1429.

James I's main contribution to the church was the donation of a chantry, a chapel designed specifically for the chanting of the Mass, and

Sailing dinghies line the shore at Blackness, Linlithgow's out port where cargo vessels once made it the second most important harbour in the whole of Scotland, second only to Edinburgh's port of Leith.

he appointed a priest, Sir William de Lany, to minister at the new altar for an annual stipend of £6 13s 4d.

King James had in the end much need of his priest's prayers because he was murdered in 1437. By then, however, it is believed that the king had had the satisfaction of seeing his palace at Linlithgow take on the shape which is so familiar today as Europe's finest courtyard palace with its open quadrangle surrounded by rooms and apartments rising to a height of four storeys. Those on the west side are believed to have remained much as they were in his day.

That Linlithgow Palace was very much habitable before his untimely death can be seen from records of purchases of quantities of paints to decorate the walls, of Arras cloth to hang on them like tapestries and of the use of no less than 111 ells of broadcloth from which to make table cloths and table napkins for the banqueting hall. An ell was an old Scottish measure for cloth, the width of the weaver's outstretched arms, and one of these metal measuring rods can still be seen displayed outside the Ell shop in the Square at Dunkeld.

James appears to have derived great delight from his new palace because it is known that he frequently rode out from Edinburgh to inspect the work in progress, and in 1428 it was sufficiently complete for him to invite and entertain important foreign visitors. They were the Archbishop of Rheims and Lord Evreux. The latter, although he had lived in France for many years, was actually the Scottish-born Sir John Stewart of Darnley, and the archbishop and he were sent specially by Charles VII to strengthen the Auld Alliance between Scotland and France by negotiating a marriage between the Dauphin, the Crown Prince of France, and James I's young daughter, the Princess Margaret.

It was her brother James who succeeded to the throne in 1437. He was too young to rule and work on the palace came to a halt during his minority. The following year in 1438 the Master of Works paid £894 10s 1d to settle outstanding accounts, but from then until 1449 there was no further major expenditure.

In 1449, however, £122 6s 6d was spent to prepare the Palace and pay for the king's honeymoon. James had married Mary, the only daughter and heiress of Arnold, Duke of Gueldres, and as it was he who established the royal tradition of gifting Linlithgow Palace as part of the queen's dowry, it was fitting that he brought his bride to the town. Their visit coincided with the Yule festivities of 1449, and this also helped establish the royal custom of often celebrating Christmas at Linlithgow.

On the whole, however, James II appears to have favoured Edinburgh and Stirling Castles as his royal residences, perhaps because he realised that they would be easier to defend, an important consideration during his turbulent reign, when he was so often challenged by his noble rivals and especially by the troublesome members of the Douglas family who were almost as powerful as he was.

Advised by Bishop Kennedy, James decided that his best chance to subdue the nobles was to divide them. Hearing that the powerful Livingstons had met in secret to plot against him, James first turned on them. This had unfortunate consequences for one of Linlithgow's best-known townsfolk, Robert Livingston, who was often known as Robyn of Linlithgow. As we saw, he succeeded Robert de Wedale as Master of Works at the Palace during the reign of James I, and by the time of James II had risen to the position of Custumar of the Customs of the Burgh. James II actually promoted him again to be Controller of the King's Household at Linlithgow, but his family's plotting was to be his undoing and he was first imprisoned at Blackness Castle and then transported to Edinburgh, where on 21st January 1450 he was executed by beheading on Castle Hill, and his lands in the parish of Linlithgow held forfeit.

Livingston was succeeded as Master of Works at the Palace by John Weir, who was one of the town's bailies and who had represented

Blackness Castle's solid Stern Tower is firmly anchored on the shore, but as Scotland's ship shape castle its Fo'csle Tower juts out into the waves as if it is ready at any moment to set sail on the next high tide.

Linlithgow by presenting the burgh accounts at the Exchequer Court in 1446 and again in 1447. He is known to have been particularly interested in the bombards, or huge cannon like Edinburgh Castle's Mons Meg, which were the latest weapons of the time, several of which he installed at Linlithgow. James II was delighted at his prowess in this field of warfare, but in 1460 it was the explosion of one of these great guns at the siege of Roxburgh Castle which cost him his life.

James left Linlithgow Palace to his widow, Mary of Gueldres, and it was here that she chose for the next three years, until her own death in 1463, to bring up her six children including the heir to the throne, the little nine-year-old James III.

Chief official at the palace at this time was Nicholas Henryson, and he was the first to be styled Keeper, rather than Master of Works. This change of title was more significant than a simple choice of words, for it appears that the palace had more or less taken shape and little work took place during his period of office, his main concern being the collection of rents from the royal lands including Bonnytoun, Kincavill, Kingsfield, Lochside and the king's acres at the east and west ends of the burgh.

1469 did, however, bring a sudden burst of expenditure on the Palace, when the by then eighteen-year-old James promised it as part of her dowry to Princess Margaret of Denmark, who in her turn gave to Scotland the islands of Orkney and Shetland as her wedding tocher.

Despite the fresh work done at the Palace, James III did not often choose to visit Linlithgow, and although some historians have suggested that the nave of St. Michael's was completed during his reign, there is no proof of this. The one long stay which James and Margaret made at Linlithgow came in 1474, when it was forced upon them by an outbreak of pestilence or plague in Edinburgh.

It was in 1474 that James III appointed one of his royal favourites, Anselm Adornes from Bruges, as Keeper of the Palace. This adventurous Fleming had befriended the young king during a visit to the royal court in Edinburgh in 1468. Officially Adornes had come over on a trade mission from the Low Countries or Netherlands, Scotland's main trading partner, but King James was much more excited to hear about the Adornes' foreign travels, especially his plans to visit the Holy Land.

As a boy James was himself desperate to travel, but was dissuaded by his parliament, which insisted that his presence in Scotland was desperately needed in these turbulent times if he was to retain his throne. Instead of travelling, James was therefore inspired to create Adornes his royal roving representative abroad and, to help ensure his safe passage in 1469, he made him a knight.

It was therefore as a Scottish lord that Adornes journeyed first to Rome and then by galley across the Mediterranean to North Africa, Egypt and finally to Jerusalem. Adornes was accompanied by his son John, who wrote a vivid description of their travels to Carthage and its ruins, to Cairo and its ancient Pyramids, and to Jerusalem and its holy places, and James was thrilled when it was presented and dedicated to him in 1471.

As a reward in 1472 Adornes was made the Scottish king's represent-ative in Burgundy and returned to the Continent until 1474. In that year he was faced with a dilemma. He was offered the position of Netherlandish Ambassador in Persia or the chance to return to Scotland as Keeper of Linlithgow Palace. Some idea of the importance of the post of Keeper of the Palace may be gained from the fact that this far-travelled man chose to take up residence in Linlithgow.

While Keeper of the Palace Adornes was responsible for rebuilding the Burgh Mill. He still travelled regularly to and from his native Netherlands, and this may have accounted for his building himself a fine house at Blackness from which he set sail on his voyages.

At Blackness, Adornes was honoured to receive a visit from his patron

King James III and probably looked forward to eventually retiring to his seaside home with its views of the Forth down which he had sailed so often on his quests for adventure. But it was not to be, because in 1483, still serving James, he braved the rigours of a Scottish January to ride to the Borders to try to achieve a reconciliation with the king's brother Albany. The many Scottish nobles, jealous of the foreigner's popularity with their king, seized their opportunity, and as he had prophesied in his will, Adornes was murdered.

His body was borne back to Linlithgow where, as he had instructed, his heart was cut out, carried to Blackness and carried home across the North Sea to his native country, where it was laid to rest beside the body of his wife in the Jerusalem Church in Bruges, which his family had built.

Adornes' royal master did not survive him long, because after six years of civil war the same rebellious Scottish nobles confronted and defeated James III at the Battle of Sauchieburn and subsequently murdered him as he hid in a nearby cottage as he tried to flee from the field.

He was succeeded by his son James IV, whose accession heralded a golden age for Scotland in which Linlithgow played a particularly glittering role as the Palace was the new monarch's favourite residence and, following Scottish royal tradition, his wedding present to his little English queen, Margaret, at the marriage of the Thistle and the Rose in 1503.

CHAPTER FOUR

Thistle, Rose and Crowns

'THE town of Linlithgow made me in the reign of the august Lord James IV.' Thus reads the inscription on the oldest of the great bells in the steeple of Linlithgow's famous kirk.

It was often the practice to install a bell to indicate the completion of a medieval church, and Linlithgow's St. Michael's, with the exception of the apse, was completed by the end of the reign of James IV, thanks in large measure to the king's own generosity, which was the trademark of the time he spent in Linlithgow.

There are many references in the records of the king's instructions to give drink silver to the masons to thank them for the work which they had done on St. Michael's, and he was equally free in his gifts to the poor whom he always welcomed to climb the steep cobbled Kirk Gate to the church and even into the Palace itself.

While James always held open house at the Palace for the poor and needy, it was on the west steps of St. Michael's that he involved them in one of the most important royal ceremonies of the year, the ceremony of the Skire Siller. This took place on Skire or Purification Thursday, the day before Good Friday, when the king took part in a service in St. Michael's similar to the annual Maundy service which Her Majesty Queen Elizabeth still attends every Easter at one of the great English cathedrals.

Just as the Queen hands out specially minted Maundy Money, so too did King James distribute Skire Siller, the little silver coins being purpose-made in Linlithgow at the royal mint, which stood on the site now occupied by the railway station. Afterwards, however, James went further by imitating the actions of Jesus at the Last Supper.

Huge basins of hot water were fetched from the Palace and liberally strewn with sweet smelling herbs by the royal servants. James then washed the feet of all the beggars and paupers who presented themselves to him, and they were no doubt many as the king also ensured that they were all provided with new suits and dresses of the best Dutch cloth as well as wooden platters and bowls from which to eat their food and sup their ale during the coming year.

While the king often celebrated Easter or Pasch at Linlithgow, it was Christmas at the Palace which he really enjoyed. For these were the Daft Days, a whole month of festivities stretching from St. Nicholas Eve on 5th December right through to Epiphany on 6th January. It is sometimes claimed that James was persuaded to copy these Christmas celebrations from the English Tudor court to help lessen the homesickness of his fourteen-year-old English bride Margaret, but the records show that the king was always willing to welcome strolling players and minstrels to Linlithgow Palace, so perhaps he needed little excuse to indulge his interests in acting, plays and music over the festive period.

When the royal party arrived at Linlithgow at the beginning of December, they always brought with them furnishings from Edinburgh, and it is said that to begin with they even brought panes of glass to fill the windows in the banqueting hall. James however is credited with 'glassynge in the great hall', and he may also have placed the first painted or stained glass in the windows of the Chapel Royal on the south side of the Palace.

Christmas at Linlithgow was very much a mixture of worship and festivities with the first celebration on St. Nicholas Eve combining both as it involved a visit to the Palace by the choir boys from the Sang School in the Kirk Gate, who first sang carols, but were thereafter entertained to a very unusual supper, for the highlight was the production of an enormous Christmas pudding or dumpling in which was hidden a single solitary bean. Each boy received a slice and the lad who was lucky enough to find the bean was given a special present by the Queen. It is said that from this simple amusement came the term 'bean feast' which is still used to this day.

Another custom connected with these past royal Christmas celebrations, the appointment of a Lord of Misrule or Abbot of Unreason, has however disappeared. This character was chosen at the St. Nicholas Eve Frolic as the first party was known, and the courtier so honoured had then to take charge of all the other entertainments for the ensuing month of Daft Days.

With a party to organise every night for a month, this must have been

Looking the full length of the Lyon Chamber, the largest fire place in Scotland can be seen. Whole tree trunks were needed to fuel all three of its large bays on nights when the entire banqueting hall was in use for feasts and frolics as during the annual Daft Days during the month long Christmas celebrations.

no small task and it was also one which taxed the ingenuity of the palace cooks who had to provide the nightly feasts with which the proceedings began. To ring the changes the cooks toiling in the cavernous stone-flagged palace kitchens, which can still be visited, often resorted to a little subterfuge. Marzipan, which had been introduced to Scotland through the German Hansa or merchant port of Lübeck in the Baltic, was a favourite ingredient for a little deception and all kinds of fruits and even imitation hardboiled eggs were often fashioned from it. Added interest was also added to the marzipan sweets by modelling them in the shapes of famous castles and palaces.

A culinary trick on an even larger scale was the creation for one of the special banquets of the legendary cockyntrice. A mysterious combination of fowl and beast, its front half consisted, as the name indicates, of a plump young cockerel to which was carefully sewn the hindquarters of a suckling pig. The whole of this creation was stuffed and then spit roasted before being gilded in egg yolks mixed with saffron and powdered ginger to creats a golden beast guaranteed to create a suitable impression at even the richest and most affluent of royal feasts.

And rich, varied and even exotic the Linlithgow Palace banquets appear to have been with the cooks able to utilise fresh ingredients from the loch and from the hunt in the surrounding hills as well as items specially imported, the records ranging from sturgeon to seal. Salmon was considered so commonplace that the palace servants are said to have protested that they should receive it no oftener than four times a week.

From Linlithgow Loch itself came trout, bream, perch and other freshwater fish and eels, while it also supplied plenty of waterfowl including wild duck, geese and swans. The swans seem often to have been substituted for the peacocks so favoured at English medieval banquets, to provide spectacular centrepieces by being carefully plucked for cooking and then all of the feathers equally carefully replaced so that they could be carried high into the Great Hall as if they were sailing in, still very much alive.

Waterfowl were by no means the only birds on the menu, others ranging from the pigeons in the doocot pie to the blackbirds which made up the ingredients of the more tactfully named colly pie. Even smaller birds such as quail and even finches were often roasted on tiny spits along with the more common barnyard fowls or chickens cooking beside the enormous kitchen fire.

Most of the spits used in the palace kitchen at Linlithgow were however much more massive, as they were used to roast whole sides of ox, sirloins of beef or haunches of venison, which were winched into position through the conveniently placed trapdoor in the centre of the large hearth. These spits required two little spit boys, young servants who did nothing but turn them all day long and baste them with gravy to ensure that they were perfectly cooked and moistly succulent for the evening feast. Being a spit boy was a very unpopular occupation, as they were scorched by the flames of the fire and half suffocated by the smoke as the fat dripped into it, despite the generosity of the king in agreeing to give them the old targets from the bow butts beside the loch which, doused in water, afforded some protection behind which to shelter. Even with this protection, however, the wee spit boys still reeked so much from the smoke that on another occasion King James gave them a special allowance to buy a second suit of clothes.

All of the palace servants, including the little spit boys, always received presents from the king and queen, not on Christmas Day but on 1st January, which although it was not celebrated as New Year's Day, which at this time came later in the spring, was suitably marked with one of the most elaborate of the feasts of the Daft Days.

No doubt this would be one of the occasions on which not a few of the nobles would seek to avail themselves of the services of the vomitorium, which can be seen in the recess opposite the fireplace of the Great Hall, which is said to be the largest in Scotland. The vomitorium consisted of a small dark chamber, much like the other garderobes or toilets which can be found at intervals around the external walls of the palace, but upon its small stone shelf were always laid ready a range of small feathers. As remove followed remove for all of twenty courses at the palace feasts, it was considered quite the done thing for the gentlemen amongst the courtiers to retire to the vomitorium, select suitable feathers, tickle the inside of the back of their throats, be violently sick and return to the long trestle tables to enjoy the remaining dishes.

From the long stone bench seats which still line the walls of the banqueting chamber and from the dimensions of this, the largest room in the Palace, it is possible to work out that a total of 350 guests could be seated for dinner. One hundred could be accommodated at each of three long tables running the full length of the hall from the buffet at the kitchen end to the raised dais at the fireplace end where the middle table formed a T with the top table at which would have been seated the royal couple and their fifty chosen courtiers. To sit below where the salt basins were situated on the three long tables was considered a distinct sign of lack of importance at the royal court, thus giving rise to the saying 'To be beneath the salt'.

On occasions of smaller gatherings only the table on the dais was used, screens being placed across the hall behind the line of the Queen's Window with its wonderful views across the loch, to ensure a more intimate setting. On these occasions also the whole fireplace was not always utilised, with the logs or coal from the pit on Bonnytoun Hill burning in the middle hearth, leaving two other arched areas below the ornate stone canopy as cosy ingleneuks, similar to those found in several of the other rooms of the Palace, where games ranging from chess and backgammon to those of a much more intimate variety could happily take place. It is interesting to note that one of the palace ingleneuks even has a ledge conveniently shaped to accommodate a glass of ale or perhaps a goblet of hot mulled wine as a suitable nightcap.

At one time the archways in the fireplace were open on both sides, allowing the heat of the flames also to warm the drawing room on the far side. It was to this room that the ladies tactfully withdrew to enable the gentlemen to enjoy their drinks and their jokes, thus giving it its name, but that came much later in the evening after the dancing and the entertainment.

James IV appears to have taken an especial interest in these royal command performances, and 'Patrik Johnson and the playaris of Lythgow' often received a summons to perform along with Blind Harry the minstrel and the court jester. Even better, however, James delighted in the occasions when troupes of circus entertainers came to Linlithgow to perform their acrobatics, sword swallowing and fire eating.

The king himself sometimes contributed to the entertainment as he was an accomplished magician, some of his less faithful courtiers even daring to suggest that behind the scenes his majesty sometimes in secret dabbled in black magic. It was true certainly that His Majesty had some unusual interests ranging from trying to find the secrets of alchemy to encouraging experiments in aviation, when the European inventor Damien tried to fly from the battlements of Stirling Castle.

At Linlithgow the offbeat interests which subsequently led to him being nicknamed 'Scotland's Most Curious King' included a fascination with wild animals, and it is known that he established a royal menagerie. At one time it included two wolves captured in Scotland for which James paid handsomely, but whether his collection ever also included a lion, thus justifying the Great Hall's other description of the Lyon Chalmer, is not known. London Zoo owes its origin to the collection of royal beasts kept originally at the Tower of London and it included several lions gifted by foreign ambassadors, so it is possible that James IV may also have received such a present and displayed it proudly in a cage at the top of the broad flight of stairs which in those days gave access to the hall. On the other hand the hall may simply have gained its title of the Lyon Chalmer from a tapestry depicting a golden lion rampant, which was at this period succeeding the silver unicorn carved in the palace's oratory as Scotland's heraldic beast.

No matter how fierce and courageous the new Scottish lion may have felt as a result of the new sense of nationhood which it had achieved during the reign of James IV and the fine new Scottish navy which he had established with the *Great Michael* as flagship to defend it, it was undoubtedly foolhardy of the king to turn against his English in-laws in a vain bid to strengthen the Auld Alliance by supporting the French in 1513.

This led to one of the most famous incidents in the whole of Linlithgow's history, the appearance of the Blue Man. Mystery has always surrounded this strange occurrence, and arguments have raged down through the centuries whether it was indeed a ghost which appeared at evensong in St. Michael's or whether it was all a carefully contrived trick designed to appeal to the king's strong belief in black magic and thought up by Queen Margaret to deter him from leading his army south to fight her English relatives.

The nearest to a contemporary account of the appearance of the Blue Man to King James as he knelt in prayer in St. Michael's on the eve of his departure is that written by Lindsay of Pitscottie, which reads as follows. 'The King came to Lithgow, where he happened to be for the time at the Council, very sad and dolorous, making his devotions to God to send him good chance and fortune in his voyage. In this meantime, there came a Man clad in a blue gown in at the kirk door and belted about him in a roll of linen cloth, a pair of brotikins on his feet to the great of his legs with all other hose and clothes conform thereto; but he had nothing on his head, but syde [long] red yellow hair behind and on his haffits [cheek blades] which went down to his shoulders, but his forehead was bald and bare. He seemed to me a man of two and fifty years with a great pike staff in his hand and came first among the Lords, crying and speiring for the King, saying he desired to speak with him. While at last he came where the King was sitting in the desk at his prayers; but when he saw the King he made him little reverence or salutation, but leaned down grofflins [gruffly] on the desk before him and said to him in this manner as follows. "Sir King, my Mother hath sent me to you, desiring you not to pass at this time where thou art purposed; for if thou does, thou wilt not fare well in the journey nor none that passeth with thee. Further she bade thee mell with no woman, nor use their counsel, nor let them touch your body nor thou theirs; for if thou do it thou will be confounded and brought to shame."

'By this man had spoken their words unto the King's Grace, the evensong was near done; and the King paused in thir words, studying to give him an answer: but in the mean time, before the King's eyes and in the presence of all the lords that were about him for the time, this man vanished away and could noways be seen nor comprehended, but vanished away as had been a blink of the sun or a whip of the whirlwind and could no more be seen. I heard say, Sir David Lindsay, Lyon Herald, and John Inglis the Marshall, who were, at that time young men and special servants to the King's Grace, were standing presently beside the King, who thought to have laid hands on this man, that they might have

Queen Margaret's Bower rises magnificently behind the Palace fountain in this unusual picture taken from one of the arrow slit windows in the turnpike stairway opposite. Sir Walter Scott romaticised the story in 'Marmion' of how Queen Margaret Tudor, wife of King James IV, dutifully climbed to this highest lookout point in the palace to watch in vain for her husband's return from ill fated Flodden Field.

speired further tidings at him: but all for nought; they could not touch him; for he vanished away betwixt them and was no more seen.'

A much more famous version of the legend of the Blue Man is provided by Sir David Lyndesay's Tale in Sir Walter Scott's *Marmion*, which describes it thus:

'In Katharine's aisle the Monarch knelt,
With sackcloth-shirt and iron belt and eyes with sorry streaming;

Around him in their stalls of state,
The Thistle Knight-Companions sate, their banners o'er them beaming.
I too was there, and sooth to tell,
bedeafened with the jangling knell, was watching where the sunbeams fell
through the stain'd casement gleaming but, while I marked what next
  befell,
It seem'd as I were dreaming.
Stepp'd from the crowd a ghostly weight, in azure gown with cincture
  white
His forehead bald, his head was bare,
down hung at length his yellow hair. —
Now mock me not, when, good my Lord I pledge to you my knightly
  word,
That, when I saw his placid grace, his simple majesty of face,
his solomn bearing, and his pace so stately gliding on, —
seemed to me ne'r did limner paint so just an image of the Saint,
who propp'd the Virgin in her faint, — the loved Apostle John.
He stepp'd before the Monarch's chair and stood with rustic plainness
there and little reverence made;
Nor head, nor body, bow'd nor bent, but on the desk his arm he leant,
And words like these he said, in a low voice, but never tone,
so thrill'd through vein, and nerve and bone:—
"My mother sent me from afar, Sir King, to warn thee not to war, —
Woe waits on thine array; If war thou wilt, of woman fair,
Her witching wiles and wanton snare,
James Stuart, doubly warned beware:
God keep thee as he may!" —
The wondering Monarch seem'd to seek for answer and found none;
And when he raised his head to speak, the monitor was gone.
The Marshall and myself had cast to stop him as he outward pass'd;
But, lighter than the whirlwind's blast, He vanished from our eyes,
Like sunbeam on the billow cast, that glances but, and dies.'

Whether or not the Blue Man was a supernatural apparition or merely
a palace servant wrapped in a blue blanket obeying Queen Margaret,
appears to have mattered little because James paid no heed to the
warning and sadly soon paid the penalty on tragic Flodden Field. Amongst
the 'Flo'ers O' the Forest', the handsome young Scottish nobles who
perished with him on this ill-fated venture, was Alexander Cornwall,
laird of Bonhard, midway between Linlithgow and Bo'ness. It is believed

that he was one of six Scottish courtiers dressed exactly like the king to try to ensure that the English did not kill the Scottish monarch. As well as their country home at Bonhard the Cornwalls owned a town house in Linlithgow High Street, and when it was modernised during the seventeenth century the centre ornament on one of the very elaborate plaster ceilings was the head of the family's hero, Alexander of Flodden fame. It is said that both Alexander and his sculptured effigy bore a striking resemblance to King James, and while this may be just a patriotic legend, it may also serve as a reminder that the Stewart kings are said to have fathered many illegitimate children at the royal court at Linlithgow. Certainly it was well known that James IV had grown tired of his little English Queen Margaret and was having many affairs at the court, hence the references in the accounts of the Blue Man to the king's unfaithfulness. It is therefore all the more surprising that Sir Walter Scott's account in *Marmion* goes on to recount that, waiting for news of the outcome of the battle, Margaret retreated to the highest point in the palace, which is still known as Queen Margaret's Bower, and wept away the weary hours waiting for her lord and master who was never to return. It was Sir Walter's famous verses which were later carved into the lintel of the door in the little vaulted chamber with its magnificent views across the Lothian countryside, and so the romantic legend was born, and to this day the thousands of tourists dutifully toil up the twisting turnpike stairs to recall it.

It was Sir Walter Scott who also paid Linlithgow the compliment of describing it in the following words:

Of all the palaces so fair, built for the royal dwelling,
In Scotland, far beyond compare, Linlithgow is excelling;

and it was James IV's successor, his son James V, who had been born at the Palace on 10th April 1512, a year before his father's death, who added the final touches to this masterpiece of Scottish building.

Amongst these was the New Entry on the south side of the Palace and the solid grey stone gatehouse which separates the outer courtyard from the Kirk Gate. Carved on it are the four honours of chivalry of which James was most proud. They include the English Order of the Garter with St. George slaying the dragon, the Order of St. Michael of France with its golden fleur de lys, and the Order of the Holy Roman Empire from Germany, with its sheep with the golden fleece as a reminder of how important the wool trade was in the Middle Ages. More interesting than these three foreign orders, however, is the inclusion second from

The impressive New Entry was added to Linlithgow Palace by King James V and may well have contributed to the famous saying accredited to his Queen, Mary of Guise, that it was more beautiful than all the chateaux in her 'belle France'. His majesty adorned the New Entry with the honours of chivalry which he held.

the left of Scotland's own order of chivalry. In his verses in *Marmion* describing the Blue Man, Sir Walter Scott mentions the famous Order of the Thistle and paints a pretty picture of the knights seated in their stalls with their banners flying, but this is probably a touch of poetic licence as no contemporary mention of a Scottish order exists. It is therefore probable that the carving of St. Andrew on his saltire, complete with surrounding thistles, on James V's gatehouse at the top of the Kirk Gate in Linlithgow, is the first evidence of the creation of a Scottish badge of chivalry and that James first awarded it to himself.

Another of the decorations with which James delighted to adorn his Palace at Linlithgow was the elaborately carved fountain in the inner courtyard whose surrounding figures are said to represent the Three Estates: the Lords, the Clergy and the Merchants.

The palace was one of the first buildings in Scotland with a piped water supply, and this was linked to the new fountain, but on festive occasions it flowed not with water but with guid red wine. Perhaps it was playing thus when it was first seen by his second wife, Mary of Lorraine or Mary of Guise as she was better known, for certainly she was duly impressed with her by then traditional royal wedding gift and promptly declared that it was far more beautiful than any of the chateaux in her belle France.

Being born at Linlithgow, James V like his Queen appears to have had a special love for the Palace. He certainly paid great attention to it, and some of the most famous stories in his life are linked to it.

Only an infant, a year and a half old when he succeeded to the throne, James spent his minority under the control of the powerful Douglas family. Much scheming took place throughout the young king's childhood, and when he was fourteen years old in 1526, Linlithgow was the scene of a determined bid to set him free organised by his mother, Chancellor Beaton and John, 3rd Earl of Lennox. Together they managed to muster an impressive army of 10,000 troops who, led by Lennox, marched towards Edinburgh.

The Douglases, who were holding James at Edinburgh Castle, learning of the advance and determined that it must be halted, ordered the Earl of Arran, who had recently come over to their side, to lead their troops out to Linlithgow.

The two sides met and faced each other on either shore of the River Avon, and so took place the Battle of Linlithgow Bridge. Lennox was handicapped by the marshy conditions on the west side of the river, and

On the top left is the insignia of the Order of the Garter, depicting St. George slaying the dragon and awarded to him by England, whose national flower the rose is shown in the chain surrounding the three lions couchant and below the English crown.

Beside it is the Scottish order of chivalry, which at the time was probably known as the Order of St. Andrew, but from which the present Order of the Thistle may trace its origins. Scotland's national flower the thistle is certainly prominent in the chain surrounding the his men were already getting the worse of the fray when the appearance of Douglas reinforcements under the Earl of Angus sent them fleeing, leaving Lennox to die on the field of battle.

Three centuries later, when the railway viaduct was being built across the valley of the Avon, several weapons were found and one of them, a sword bearing the Latin motto, 'Pono leges virtute', 'I maintain the laws of valour' on one side of the blade, was displayed for many years in Victorian times in the Council Chamber of the Town House. Lord Lennox and his brave but vain effort to regain power for the royal house of Stewart is commemorated in Linlithgow by the place name Lennox Gardens given to the small housing development on the north side of the approach road to Linlithgow Bridge where the battle took place all those years ago.

Two years later in 1528, James V·was sixteen and old enough to assume control in his own right, but he never managed to master the rival Scottish nobles as his father had done. He was forced therefore to rely heavily on support from the church, and he in turn remained faithful to it despite the rumblings of the coming Reformation. But James was not blind to the shortcomings of the priests, the monks and the nuns and tried to get them to improve their ways and keep their vows. One way he did this was to encourage his former tutor, Sir David Lyndsay of the Mount, to write *Ane Satyre of the Thrie Estatis*. A special play, masque or mime was always performed at the Palace to mark the end of the Daft Days at Epiphany, and so just as Shakespeare's *Twelfth Night* was first performed at the English court on such an occasion, Lyndsay's masterpiece was first staged at Linlithgow Palace on 6th January 1540. If by any chance the clergy in the royal audience in the Great Hall had failed to grasp the point of the play, King James himself is said to have added to it by addressing them all at the close of the performance, but in the end to no avail.

---

proud lion rampant beneath the Scottish crown and above the figure of St. Andrew on his distinctive Saltire cross.

In the middle is the Order of the Golden Fleece which was awarded by the Holy Empire, the golden ram indicating the important part which the wool trade played in the creation of wealth in the world of the Middle Ages.

On the right is the Order of St, Michael awarded by Scotland's auld ally France and appropriately right next to the church, depicting St. Michael overcoming evil in the shape of a dragon. In the centre beneath the French crown are three lilies while set into the chain can be seen the gold cockle shells which early pilgrims used to carry as symbols of good luck on their long and often dangerous journeys to the holy places.

Like his father, James loved the theatre and acting, and it is said often went among his people in disguise. He also liked swapping roles, it would appear, when the royal court was at Linlithgow. Tradition has it that James grew tired of the daily receptions which he was expected to hold each morning in the Presence Chamber with its famous ladder window casting the pattern of a double rainbow on the tiled floor. It is said therefore that one day the king arranged to change places with his favourite servant at Linlithgow, the famous Rab Gibb, who during his years at the Palace is said to have filled many roles from that of stirrup man to the king to that of court jester.

At first, though, Rab played the part of His Majesty seriously, listening intently to the many requests for royal favours and grants of land, until he too became utterly bored with the proceedings and brought them to an end by demanding, 'Awa, awa ye greedy loons and bring me here my ain true and trusty frien' Rab Gibb, the only man at my court who serves me from stark love and kindness'.

James was seemingly so impressed with this wit and with Rab's performance that he rewarded him with the estate of Caribber on the banks of the River Avon, to the west of Linlithgow on the road to Armadale, where Rab subsequently built his castle. In addition the story became so well known throughout the land that the saying 'For stark love and kindness' was often engraved on engagement and wedding rings, on heart-shaped brooches and on snuff boxes, where it appeared under the symbol of two clasped hands.

Brooches and trinkets such as this were often sold at the luckenbooths, the locked booths, which were a feature of most Scottish markets such as those held several days each week around Linlithgow's Cross Well, of which nearby Market Lane is still a reminder. Most of the items on sale at the Linlithgow markets came, however, from the surrounding country-side, the drovers with their beasts and the farmers with their merchandise having to wait outside the Westport, Lowport, High or Eastport until they opened at daybreak to come into town to set up their stalls. For Linlithgow was very much a walled town at this time and the townsfolk slept all the sounder in their beds at night as they knew that from the curfew, the signal to put out the fires (from the French 'couvre le feu') at dusk until the following dawn, the town's gates or ports were all well barred and bolted.

Fragments of the ancient town wall can still be found along Union Road, but most of it was destroyed by the coming of the railway in 1842. Another reminder of the medieval days when Linlithgow slept snug

The off-shoots of Katie Wearie's tree still provide welcome shade for passers-by at West Port. Across the street where gates once guarded the entrance to the town can be seen two of Linlithgow's oldest hostelries, the West Port Hotel and the white washed Black Bitch Tavern.

behind its wall and gates is Katie Wearie's tree, or rather the carefully tended offshoots from the original, whose leaves still provide shade each spring and summer. For according to tradition, it was always at this spot at the junction of Mains Road and Falkirk Road that drover Katie chose to sit and rest while she waited for the gates to open on market morns.

Tradition also has it that while Katie watered her cattle at the horse trough which long existed at the point where the zebra crossing now replaces it in this modern age, she often also bathed her tired feet. Most travellers, on reaching the West Port, however, appear to have preferred to refresh their throats rather than their toes, because it was here that two of Linlithgow's best-known hostelries, the Black Bitch and the West Port, both flourished.

But not all visitors were always welcome to Linlithgow because, given the town's reputation as a healthy place, the magistrates were determined to keep it so. The main threat to Linlithgow's clean bill of health was always seen as Borrowstounness, the Burgh Town On The Point or

Bo'ness as it later became known for short, the upstart port three miles to the north on the River Forth. Unlike its own port at neighbouring Blackness, Linlithgow always bitterly resented that it had no control over what went on at Bo'ness and complained frequently that without its wise guidance quarantine restrictions were usually ignored to boost trade by ensuring ships got a fast turn round, thus risking outbreaks of plague and pestilence. Furious that their protests were ignored, the Linlithgow magistrates ordered that a gallows be built at the West Port and warned that any Bo'nessian who dared venture over The Flints, the 500-foot-high hill between the two towns, while there was plague in the port, would be arrested on sight and made to 'jouk the gibbet'.

The Linlithgow magistrates were equally protective of Linlithgow's boundaries and so grew up the town's famous custom of Riding the Marches. From as early as Linlithgow's receiving its royal charter in 1389 it seems likely that an annual inspection was made on foot, but the first actual riding is believed to have taken place towards the end of the reign of James V in 1541. This innovation, which has remained such a popular and colourful feature of the town's life ever since, is usually credited to Linlithgow's first Provost, Henry Forest of Magdalenes.

As a date for this first Riding of the Marches, Provost Forest chose Easter Tuesday 1541, probably for reasons both of religion and weather. The weather seems likely to have persuaded the Provost to wait long enough into spring to ensure the likelihood of a reasonable day and reasonable underfoot conditions, but not too long so that any damage caused by winter storms could be put right without overlong delay. Religion seems to have influenced the choice of a date in Holy Week because, as with the rogation ceremonies in England, part of the original Riding of the Marches included the blessing of the bounds by a priest.

While the religious element was similar to that involved in beating the bounds of English medieval towns, much to the relief no doubt of the local bairns the Linlithgow Riding of the Marches never seems to have included the painful process of bending the children over the boundary stones and whipping them with long canes, the adults in Scotland preferring instead to refresh their own memories by having a drink at each spot. As the first Riding fell during Lent, it was not possible for the Provost and the other participants, upon their return to the Town House, to follow their drinks with a good meal, far less a feast, and it may have been this factor which soon led future Marches to be held later on the Tuesday after Whitsun, when a fair was also held at the Cross. The Riding of the Marches continued to be celebrated annually on this date for over two hundred years, until in 1767 the Provost, Magistrates and Councillors decided without explanation to move the Whitsun Fair to the second Thursday in June, Marches Day itself to be on the following Tuesday, and so it has been ever since.

A look at those who rode the Marches in these early years provides a great deal of information about the 2,500 or so inhabitants who lived in the town in the Middle Ages, as all of Linlithgow's Trade Guilds and Incorporated Crafts were represented. The original eight, whose membership and functions are explained below, were the Hammermen, the Wrights, the Baxters, the Coopers, the Weavers, the Tailors, the Cloth Fullers and the Cordiners. Around the middle of the sixteenth century the Fleshers, who were always a large and important group in Linlithgow, managed to obtain the status of an Incorporated Guild and replaced the Guild of Fullers or Waulkers as the number of cloth finishers working in the town was apparently declining.

The Incorporated Guild of Hammermen embraced all of the craftsmen in Linlithgow who worked in any form of metal, from blacksmiths to gold- and silversmiths. They included the farriers who made the horseshoes, the armourers who made swords, pikes and other weapons, and the workers at the royal mint. The only metal workers who were not allowed membership of the Hammermen's Guild were those who worked in tin, because they were, of course, the much despised tinkers. The tinkers had a bad reputation because they roamed from town to town knocking on doors seeking pans to mend and knives to grind and allegedly used the knowledge of the houses they visited to return to steal and commit other petty crimes. Either because of this rejection or perhaps for their own protection, Linlithgow's tinkers lived together in what must have been very overcrowded conditions in the little two-storeyed, red pantile-roofed stone cottage the ruins of which can still be seen behind the Armoury pub on the north side of the west end of the High Street. In their crowded cottage, the tinkers slept in the low-ceilinged attic below the eaves and both lived and worked downstairs. When they finished work they must often naturally have sought a drink at the Armoury, or the Swan, as the beautiful mosaic white swan at the entrance reminds us it was originally and much more appropriately called, but this caused even more trouble for the tinkers. For the Swan was traditionally the home of the Guild of Wrights who, like all of Linlithgow's guilds and incorporated crafts, had their headquarters in an inn or pub, and they insisted that they wanted nothing to do with unwelcome tinkers, who they maintained should drink with the smiths and other metal workers

This four storey high town house, which stood on the site of Linlithgow Railway Station was always reputed locally to have been the royal mint. In the middle ages the mint moved from town to town along with the royal court so that the king could keep a tight personal control of the coinage. The Skire Siller, the Scottish version of Maundy Money, which King James IV dispensed to the poor people of Linlithgow from the steps of St. Michael's on the Thursday before Good Friday may well have been minted here.

where they met at the other end of the High Street at the Golden Lion, which like the old Swan still exists, but again with a change of name, to the Red Lion.

The Wrights included all of Linlithgow's wood workers from wheel wrights to cart wrights and from joiners to cabinet makers or undertakers. Like all of the guilds, the Wrights, as well as using their pub as a place to meet and drink, used it to hold their weekly meetings at which they were presided over by their Deacon and at which business such as the admission of apprentices, standards of goods and prices were all discussed and agreed. Decisions reached were later conveyed to the rest of the townsfolk through the Deacons' Court at which all eight Deacons met regularly. It is interesting to note that Deacons still ride the Marches and that despite the creation of a Community Council under the local government re-organisation of 1975, the Deacons' Court still meets regularly and thumbs its collective nose at authority by proudly and defiantly appointing a Provost.

In the past all of Linlithgow's guilds had this same guid conceit of themselves, and none more so than the Baxters or bakers, who also included the town's brewers and innkeepers, all of whom prided themselves on the quality of the fare which they provided, as the kean and Oliphant families of bakers still do to this day. Market days were of course particularly busy for the members of the Baxters' Guild with their mutton pies and mutton and onion pies amongst the earliest examples of carry-out food in Scotland, their water pastry shells specially designed to make them strong enough to eat in the hand, accompanied no doubt by a pint of ale or a glass of whisky.

Beer and whisky were products long manufactured in Linlithgow, with the Guild of Coopers being kept busy supplying barrels for the town's breweries and the famous St. Magdalene's Distillery, whose sadly long-disused premises still form a prominent landmark on the Edinburgh Road.

Linlithgow always had links with the textile trades, with no fewer than three guilds representing their workers, the Guild of Weavers, the Guild of Tailors and the Guild of Fullers or Waulkers as they were often called because of one of the processes used in finishing the cloth. They also included in their membership the Litsters as the Dyers were originally known.

It was most likely through its weavers that Linlithgow got its own traditional tune, 'The Roke and the Wee Pickle Tow' without the playing of which no Marches Morn would be complete. For although it is

The steep Kirk Gate leading to the Palace and St. Michael's Church is one of Linlithgow's most historic thoroughfares. While Kirk Gate is the usual spelling of this old place name it is also suggested that it may at one time have been spelt Kirk Gait as in Lang Gait, the old name for Princes Street before the development of Edinburgh's Georgian New Town and meaning the walk or stride up to the church on the hill.

A suggestion that the Kirk Gate's ancient retaining walls should be breached to enable tourist buses to reach the Palace was decisively rejected as destroying the very thing which visitors to Linlithgow come to admire.

sometimes given the more dignified title of 'Lord Lithgow's March' 'The Roke' is essentially a weaving tune and with Linlithgow's long connection with the textile trade it is probable that this is how the tune became so closely associated with the town. Originally however it appears to have been written by an Aberdeenshire schoolmaster, Alexander Ross, who was dominie of the little village school at Kincardine O'Neil for 36 years during the 18th century. Ross was born in Torphins in 1699 and died at Lochee in Forfarshire in 1784. He published the 'Roke' in 1768 in a song book called 'Helenore or the Fortunate Shepherdess', which was printed in Aberdeen. It must have proved popular for eight years later in 1776 it was republished in 'Herd's Collection'.

Originally 'The Roke' was much longer than it is today, with no fewer than 19 verses each of 8 lines, but subsequent books abbreviated it to the first and final three verses as is played and sung today.

'THE ROKE AND THE WEE PICKLE TOW'

There was an auld wife had a wee pickle tow
And she wad gae try the spinnin o't,
But lootin her down, her rock took a low
And that was a bad beginnin' o't.
She sat and she grat, and she flat, and she flang,
And she threw and she blew, and she wriggled and wrang,
And she chokit and bakit, and cried like to mang,
Alas for the dreary beginnin' o't.

I've wanted a sark for these auchty years and ten,
And this was to be the beginnin' o't,
But I vow I shall want it for as long again,
Or ever I try the spinnin' o't,
For never since ever the ca'd as they ca'me
Did sic a mishap and mischanter befa' me,
But she shall ha'e leave baith to hand and to draw me
The neist time I try the spinnin' o't.

I ha'e keepit my hoose now these three score o'years
And aye kept frae the spinnin' o't,
But how I was sarkit, foul fa' them that speirs
For it minds me o' the beginnin' o't.
But oor women are now-a-days a' grown sae brae
That ilka ane maun ha'e a sark, and some ha'e two —
The warld was better when ne'er ane ava,
Had a rag but ane at the beginnin' o't.

In the days they ca' yor gin auld folks could but get
To a surcoat, hough-syde, for the winnin' o't,
Of coat-raips weel cut by the cast o' their shape,
They never socht mair o' the spinnin' o't,

A pair o' grey toggers weel clinkit benew,
Of nae other lit but the hue of the ewe,
With a pair of rough mullions to scruff through the dew;
Was the fee they socht at the beginnin' o't.

But we maun ha'e linen, and that maun ha'e we,
And how get ye that but by spinnin' o't,
How can we ha'e face for to seek a great fee,
Except that we can help at the winnin' o't.
And we ha'e pearlies and marbles, and locks,
And some other things the ladies ca' smocks,
And how get we that gin we tak nee o'er rocks,
And pu' what we can at the spinnin' o't.

'Tis needless for us to mak' our remarks,
Fae our mithers miss-cookin' the spinnin' o't,
She never kenn'd ocht, o' the guid o' the sarks
Frae this a-back tae the beginnin' o't.
Twa three 'ell o' plqidin' was a' that bude be bocht,
For in ilka town sic an things was no' wrocht,
Sae little they kenn'd o' tha spinnin' o't.

Rock or Roke means the wooden distaff used in spinning. Pickle means a small quantity. Tow is hemp in an unprepared state. Lout means to bend and low is a flame.

According to Stenhouse in his notes to Johnston's Musical Museum, 'The Roke' existed in an earlier state, whose 'rather crude words' were cleaned up by Ross and this may well be true as the tune appears to have been known as early as 1724 when it is mentioned in 'Ramsay's Tea Table Miscellany'.

Versions of 'The Roke' are said to exist as far away as Burgandy in France, but no matter what its origins it is very definitely Linlithgow's and its familiar jaunty tune is heard over and over again throughout the town on Marches Morn.

Returning to the Guilds, the last of the original eight incorporated crafts of Linlithgow were the Cordiners, who included all those who worked in leather, including tanners, glovers, harness makers, saddlers and shoemakers or snabs as they were known locally and who became very important in the town during the seventeenth and eighteenth centuries. Several reminders of Linlithgow's links with the leather industry can still be seen, including the metal runners in one of the pends leading down to the lochside tanneries which made it easier to move the very heavy bundles of hides. The tanneries themselves were all on the lochside because of the need for plentiful supplies of fresh water, but most of the leather workers seem to have had their homes on the opposite side of the High Street where place names such as Tanners Wynd and Cordiners Land are still a reminder of them. For the tanning process, as well as water, large quantities of oak leaves and bark were also required, and as well as the place name Birkhill, the oak wreath carved round the badge of the Cordiners above the door of Number 125 on the south side of the High Street recalls this connection. It is interesting to note that as late as 1871 the census recorded four shoemakers and a leather worker living at this address. Further west, still on the south side of the High Street, the Cordiners' sign of a leather worker's awl can again be seen incorporated in the stained glass of the Crown Inn, where they had their headquarters, and also on the inn's sign, where the liberty had been taken to replace the oak garland with Scottish thistles.

Originally the fleshers who slaughtered the beasts to obtain the hides for the Cordiners appear to have been members of their guild but, as already mentioned, by the time of James V and the middle of the 1500s they had grown greatly in importance and soon afterwards replaced the cloth finishers as the eighth incorporated trade. In their guild they in turn included the town's butchers and also the glue makers who used up all the bones and horns which would otherwise have gone to waste. The quality of Linlithgow glue was so well known that the Royal Company of Archers insisted in Victorian times that it be used to make their bows and to stick the feathers to their arrows. The Stein family's Gowan Stank Glue Works, which stood on the site now occupied by St. Joseph's Primary School on Preston Road, continued in production until 1958 and its tall chimney was a well-known landmark, but even better known was its smell which well lived up to its name and which was always said to alert rail travellers from the west to the fact that they were nearing Linlithgow Station.

The Fleshers were always associated with the west end of the town, where the well-known Henderson family still operate their modern abbatoir, and conveniently chose the Black Bitch Tavern as their headquarters. The Black Bitch, which is now owned by the popular Hardy family, is believed to be the oldest hostelry in Linlithgow. It takes its name from the famous black greyhound bitch which, according to local legend, devotedly swam out with food to its master, who had been held tied to an oak tree on one of the islands in Linlithgow Loch. The greyhound is of course commemorated to this day by the fact that natives of Linlithgow are proud to shock outsiders by always calling themselves Black Bitches and by the fact that the Black Bitch tethered to an oak tree is one of the town's two official coats of arms. It is this coat of arms which now appears as the sign for the Black Bitch Tavern, but originally its sign recognised its connections with the Fleshers who met and drank there, because it was in the shape of a butcher's slab with a crossed knife and cleaver painted on it. A real butcher's stone slab also used to sit on the pub counter until lost following a fire in the 1930s when the Black Bitch where Bob Hardie is now mine host, was owned by the Ingram family. According to them, the slab had the date 1284 carved on it and they also had this date recorded on the inn sign as a reminder that the historic Black Bitch may well be the oldest drinking howff in Scotland.

All eight of Linlithgow's incorporated trades kept a strict monopoly on their trades, regulating admission of apprentices, their promotion after they had served their time — usually a period of at least five years — to craftsmen, the entry of qualified craftsmen from other towns, the fixing of wages, the payment of dues, methods of manufacture, the quality of the goods and prices charged to customers. Together they guarded their privileges and promptly suppressed any attempt by an outsider to manufacture or even try to sell any goods anywhere within the burgh boundaries. Together they also built, maintained and operated the Guildry, the massive stone-walled warehouse on the shore at the end of the pier at Blackness, where they could safely store their goods until a ship was ready to export them to England or the Continent and where they could also store imported raw materials until they could transport them to Linlithgow. The ruins of the Guildry survived until the 1960s when they were hauled down to make way for a modern block of council flats, which now mars the whole appearance of the Square at Blackness. To add insult to injury, it even bears the old name of the Guildry.

Each of the eight guilds also supported one of the altars in St. Michael's, paying for the candles which burned on them and for the priests to say Mass. These altars occupied each of the spaces between the huge stone pillars of the nave as well as the transepts and numbered at least twenty-four.

The snabs or cobblers supported two altars, those to St. Stephen and St. Crispin. The coopers paid for the altar to St. Cuthbert and the hammermen maintained an altar to St. Eloy who, as he had been a goldsmith, was very appropriately their patron saint. Other altars in St. Michael's were dedicated to St. Michael as patron saint of the church, to

King James V, father of Mary Queen of Scots, added the famous ornate fountain to the courtyard of Linlithgow Palace thus providing it with its crowning glory. The triple tiered fountain is said to have flowed with wine on the nights of the many feasts which were held in the magnificent Lyon Chamber, whose windows dominate the eastern facade behind it.

the Virgin Mary, who had two altars, to the Holy Trinity, to the Holy Cross or Holy Rood, to the Holy Blood, to Corpus Christi, to John the Baptist, to Saint Saviour, to St. John the Evangelist, to St. Peter, St. Andrew, St. Brigid or St. Bryde who was patron saint of the Hamiltons of Kinneil and who is still remembered on their lands at East Kilbride, the new town near their principal seat at Hamilton, to St. Peter, to St. Anne, to St. Ninian, to St. Katherine (sometimes spelt with a C), to St. Nicholas, to St. Syth, to St. Anthony, and, finally, to All Saints.

To keep the very necessary support of the Church, James V appears to have had to go along with a policy of persecution of any would-be reformers, especially after Cardinal Beaton gained power in 1539. After the execution of the Sheriff of Linlithgow, Sir James Hamilton of Finnart, who was accused of trying to murder the king by shooting at him from the Palace and from the steeple of St. Michael's, James became very troubled and suffered from terrible visions, including the famous night when James roused the whole of Linlithgow Palace, declaring that he had been haunted by the ghost of the Justice Clerk, Thomas Scot. In his *History of the Reformation*, John Knox described the scene as follows:

'How terrible a vision the said Prince was lying in Linlithgow that night Thomas Scot died in Edinburgh, men of good credit can yet report. For afraid at midnight or after, he called aloud for torches and raised all that lay beside him in the Palace and told that Scot had been at him with a company of Devils'.

Three years later James was defeated by the English at the Battle of Solway Moss in 1542 and, sore depressed, retreated to Falkland Palace in Fife. There the news which reached him on a cold December day brought by a rider on horseback from Linlithgow Palace did nothing to cheer him, and he died before the year was out. "It cam' wi a lass and it will gang wi' a lass", were said to be his dying words, when told that his wife had given birth to a daughter.

CHAPTER FIVE

Birth Place Of A Queen

LINLITHGOW'S claim to world wide historic fame is undoubtedly in its being the birthplace of Mary Queen of Scots. She was born on December 8th 1542 at Linlithgow Palace, probably in the royal apartment, the inner most room of the royal suite in the west wing of the Palace, which is said to be the finest royal suite in Europe. As was the custom of the time, the infant Mary's first outing would be to her christening but whether it took place in the Palace's own Chapel Royal or across the outer courtyard in St. Michael's is not certain.

While Mary's birth in the Palace has brought the town fame, Linlithgow actually saw less of her than of previous Stewart monarchs. The Parliament which followed the death of her father James V agreed that Mary should either stay at Linlithgow or at Stirling Castle as the Queen Mother preferred, but the famous 'Rough Wooing' by the English King Henry VIII during which he sent his fleet into the River Forth, convinced Cardinal Beaton and the Earl of Arran that Mary was no longer safe in Scotland and should be sent to France.

She left behind a country in turmoil as the Lords of the Reformation broke from the Catholic Church. It was a break away challenged in Linlithgow by the local teacher, the well educated Rector of the Grammar School, Ninian Winzet, who just like the late king James V, was convinced that the Roman Catholic Church could be saved by being reformed from within. Winzet debated ably with John Knox and refused steadfastly to yield to his opponents but in the end was forced to give up his school and flee to Germany. There his talents were recognised and he went on to greater things as Bishop of Ratisbon.

The Reformation tore Linlithgow apart with equally devoted followers on both sides. The first martyr of the Reformation, Patrick Hamilton, was a descendant of the Hamiltons of Kinscavill and the family forfeited their estate in support of the cause. He was followed to the stake by another native of Linlithgow, Henry Forrest, who also chose to die for his faith. His family had owned St. Magdalenes estate for several generations and had loyally supported St. Michael's Church as well, of course as supplying the town with its first provost.

In 1559 Reformation fever seized Scotland and on 29th June the Lords of the Congregation descended on Linlithgow to cleanse not only St. Michael's but the Chapel Royal in the Palace itself. Systematically they smashed the altars and the holy water stoops and every statue of every saint which they could find. In the Chapel Royal the empty niches still bear silent testimony to their official vandalism, the quality of the carving of the little stone cherubs, each playing a different musical instrument, alone remains as evidence of the magnificence of the workmanship which they must have destroyed in the name of ridding these places of worship of anything which reminded them of papacy, and the idolatrous worship of saints. In the Palace they even attacked the statues in the courtyard and in St. Michael's only the statue of St. Michael himself survived, not because the Protestant Lords had any greater respect for him than for any of the other 'painted idols', but because the patron saint of the church was so well built into the outer fabric of the church that to have removed him would have brought down the south west corner of the building. Instead as can be seen to this day the Reformers had to be content with clipping St. Michael's wings.

Inside the church too there were many changes. All of the altars were swept away and with them went the short services of the Masses which the townsfolk had been used to attending. So short had been these Masses that most worshippers could stand throughout the worship, only a stone seat round the outside edge of the church being provided for the old or ill, thus giving rise to the saying 'Let the weak go to the wall'. Now with the much much longer Protestant services with their very lengthy sermons, pews became necessary for the first time. There was plenty of space to accommodate them where the altars had formerly been, but what shape they should be and who should pay for their installation caused much controversy in the town. In one case the magistrates objected because the Guild of Tailors built their pew higher than any other in the whole church because they claimed that their guild was the most important in the town. The tailors ignored the protest by the bailies and went on to decorate their pew with an enormous pair of shears and a

The famous Queens' Pulpit in St. Michael's with the intricately carved figure of Mary Queen of Scots standing immediately below the unusual pulpit fall designed and made by members of the congregation. The other queens carved in two of the other niches of the pulpit are Queen Margaret later Saint Margaret, whose chapel can be visited at Edinburgh Castle and Queen Victoria. The fourth niche has still to be filled.

huge smoothing iron. This brought an even more indignant protest especially as the tailors' pew was immediately opposite the royal throne.

Establishing new rules for the new Protestant regime proved taxing for the Provost and the bailies but any hope that the guilds had that they might escape paying their dues for the altars which had all been swept away were soon dispelled when they were informed that as the light in the church came from the windows instead of the candles they must each contribute towards the maintenance of the glass! The Fraternity of Hammermen did not take kindly to this new ruling and decided to try to evade it by employing a mason to build up their window with stone! The Provost and Bailies were furious at this cheek and promptly ordered the smiths to get the mason back again to remove all the stone and replace the glass.

The Linlithgow magistrates also kept a close check on the standard of workmanship at St. Michael's and on one occasion sacked a slater because the roof which he was supposed to have repaired was leaking and letting in the rain and the damp was threatening to rot the fine oak ceiling, which was at that time one of the church's finest features.

Sometimes, however, their reasons for dismissing a tradesman do not seem to have been so sound. Such is the case of Thomas Mastertoun who was sacked because 'he done wrang to James Glen, Bailie, in not acknowledging him on the market cross and not giving him reverence'.

On the whole however the magistrates of Linlithgow acted wisely and saved St. Michael's from the worst excesses of the Reformation. The Protestants had a rather strange view about the sanctity of the church claiming that it was only the actual area used for services which was sacred but while the magistrates allowed the temporary storage of 'forty great trees and twa hundred deals', which were waiting to be used for the repair of the Town House, or the Tolbooth as it was described on this occasion, they steadfastly drew the line at permanently partitioning the nave from the rest of the church. Thus unlike other historic churches such as St. Mary's at Haddington and Paisley Abbey, St. Michael's thankfully remained intact.

Mary returned to Scotland in 1561 and three weeks after landing at Leith paid her first visit to Linlithgow on 11th September, accompanied by many of the French courtiers and servants whom she had brought with her. According to local tradition Mary and her followers appear to have enjoyed their visit because she is said to have played some of the first games of golf in Scotland in the grounds of the Peel (having brought the game back with her from the continent, where it had been invented in Holland) and she also enjoyed French style picnics in the surrounding countryside or 'en la campagne' thus giving Champany on the road to Blackness its unusual name.

Champany was not the only French placename which Mary and her royal court are believed to have given to the Linlithgow district. The Queen and her friends all rode to their picnics and as the stables in the north wing of the Palace were never adequate to house most of the horses, they had to be brought in from grazing pastures to the east of the town near Bridgend where to this day the placename Champfleurie now the home of Mr. Kerr still provides a reminder of this 'flowery field'.

In the centre of Linlithgow too the Vennel is a reminder of days during Mary's reign when local bairns were almost all likely to be commanded to 'venez vite' or to 'allez' as they were ordered to come or to go. In the 1500s as well as the Vennel which still exists today, the town also had a South Vennel which ran behind the old town wall from Edinburgh Road in the

The courtyard at Champany Inn, which takes its unusual name from the days when Mary Queen of Scots and her French courtiers used to ride out from Linlithgow Palace to picnic, 'a la champagne'. All these centuries later Champany with its far famed cuisine still manages to retain a distinctly French country air, with its red pantiled roof, its white washed walls and its tables outdoors in the paved courtyard.

east to Preston Road and the bridle track over the hills to Bathgate in the west.

Within the town wall, the Linlithgow of this period was very typical of a small compact Scottish burgh. The three Ports: West, Low, High or East, again with their French connection, have already been mentioned as has the High Street which, as today, ran the full length of the town and connected them. Behind each house, on either side of the High Street, lay its garden. Long and narrow, especially as many of the houses were built Dutch style gable on to the street, these were known as the run riggs and Linlithgow is the last remaining town where this ancient form of agriculture can still be seen in an urban setting. To the south these long strips of gardens ran right up to the town wall and to the north they ran right down to the lochside.

On the south side of the High Street, St. Michael's Wynd or Easter Wynd ran between the run riggs to the town wall, but Lion Well Wynd,

Dog Well Wynd and New Well Wynd were not yet in existence, the life of the town centring on the Cross Well to which all of the housewives and lassies had to come to get their pitchers filled with water. Around it too, and along Market Lane to the east from where the road continued round to the original entrance to the Palace, clustered the traders' stalls, while the shops in the High Street were themselves little more substantial as they consisted mainly of timber booths projecting out into the street.

Behind the Cross Well stood the original Tolbooth, which was replaced by the present Town House the building of which was completed in 1670. There the Provost and Bailies met regularly and as magistrates duly meted out justice, their sentences of scourgings with the long leather lash and brandings with the town's 'L' shaped brand being immediately and publicly executed in full public view as a deterrent to others at the Cross.

As well as its own distinctive brand, Linlithgow was also famous for possessing its own full set of measures for weight, volume and length, before such things were standardised throughout Scotland and these can still be seen on display in the Royal Scottish Museum in Edinburgh's Chamber Street, although many people feel that they should by rights be returned for exhibition in the town where they belong. Proposals to start a burgh museum in Annet House are, however, still simply proposals thanks to the apparent indifference of West Lothian District Council many of whose members seem to fear that any museum would be an unwelcome reminder of the days when Linlithgow was truly West Lothian's county town rather than Bathgate to which they have retreated.

While Annet House on the south side of the High Street would make a welcome museum it is not itself nearly as old as several of the other houses which still exist, such as the National Trust's Hamilton's Land tenement and West Port House, which dates back to Queen Mary's reign. West Port House is a typical Scottish 16th century thick stone walled 'L' shaped mansion and has only recently been converted into flats.

Next door to West Port House, to the east, stood Bein Castle, which still survives as a place name, but how it was originally derived is a mystery suggestions ranging from the links with St. Nicholas Bean Frolic at the Palace to a link with Gaelic Ben or Bein meaning a hill as it does stand at the top of a slight rise in the High Street.

Along the length of the High Street in Queen Mary's time styles and quality of property must have varied greatly the substantial stone built slate roofed homes of the Spanish and French Ambassadors and the

The French Ambassador's House, which stood four storeys high opposite Old County Buildings was one of many fine medieval town houses swept away to make way for the modern Vennel Flats. Its narrow frontage to the High Street, similar to many Dutch houses, was typical of Scottish town architecture of its period, as were its red pantiled roof and steep crow stepped gable.

Rear view of the French Ambassador's House taken shortly before its demolition in the 1960's shows how overgrown and run down this part of the High Street had become, but with hindsight much could have been done to restore this historic home and its neighbours.

town houses of the many nobles being interspersed with much humbler single storeyed cottages many with thatched roofs.

Life too in Linlithgow must have been very stratified with distinct differences in life style between the courtiers, the merchants and ministers who by then formed the middle class and the poor who, if they were servants, at least had a roof over their heads but who in many cases appear to have lived rough.

For the lords, their ladies and their families, on the other hand, 16th century Linlithgow offered many leisure opportunities. Apart from fishing in the loch, hunting in the Bathgate Hills and riding in the surrounding countryside the Palace is recorded as possessing its own bowling green, which occupied the site where the entrance lodge beside the Ooter or Outer Entry at the top of the Kirk Gate is now situated. There are also references to the King's tennis court, which is believed to have occupied a site adjacent to the bowling green and must have been similar to the early form of real or royal tennis court with its wooden balconies which still survives at Falkland Palace in Fife.

Evidence of one sport which still exists in the grounds of the Peel was archery which was practised daily at the bow butts overlooking the loch. It was, of course, very important that the nobles and their sons perfected the martial arts and this was also encouraged at the Royal Court in Linlithgow by the holding of tournaments. The tournament field was situated at the west end of the town at Linlithgow Bridge, where two local place names, Justinhaugh and Listloaning are still a reminder of the horseback jousting which took place in the lists in front of the Scottish royal family.

Apart from her first stay at Linlithgow, after her return from France, Mary Queen of Scots paid three other visits of particular interest. In 1565 she and her second husband, Lord Darnley, stayed at the Palace while marching west to Glasgow to put down the revolt of the Protestant Lords led by the Earl of Moray. Less than two years later it was with Darnley that Mary had quarrelled following his involvement in the brutal murder of her Italian favourite David Rizzio, but officially they were together again when they spent their last night together at Linlithgow on 28th January 1567. Darnley was by then a sick man and to all intents and purposes Mary was acting as a caring and sympathetic wife as she escorted her husband back to Edinburgh. Next day, however, on arrival back in the city, Mary appears to have made a suitable excuse why Darnley should not accompany her back to Holyrood and left him lodged instead at Kirk o' Field House (on the site where Edinburgh

University Old Quad now stands) and where in the early hours of the following morning he was murdered by strangulation before the house was blown up in a clumsy attempt to cover up the deed.

Darnley's death was linked to Mary's new lover, Lord Bothwell, and it is interesting that the queen's final stay at Linlithgow two months later on 23rd April 1567 was the night before her willing abduction by him. That night Bothwell's messenger, Ormiston, came in secret to the Queen at the Palace so that she was well prepared for Bothwell's sudden appearance when she reached the other side of the River Almond on her way back to Edinburgh.

Mary's subsequent imprisonment in Loch Leven Castle followed by her escape and flight to England, resulted in the appointment of her half brother, James Stewart, Earl of Moray as Regent and to one of the most famous events to occur in Linlithgow in the sixteenth century. As a Protestant, Moray had many enemies amongst the Catholic population and one Catholic with a particular grudge was James Hamilton of Bothwellhaugh. As a loyal Catholic he had supported Mary at the Battle of Langside in 1568 and after the defeat was one of those punished by Moray, who ordered the confiscation of all of his lands.

Bitter with resentment young Hamilton waited for an opportunity to seek his revenge until early in 1670 he heard that the Regent would leave Linlithgow on either January 22nd or 23rd. Hamilton approached the leaders of the Catholic opposition party and persuaded them to allow him to hide in the Linlithgow town house belonging to the Archbishop of St. Andrews. The Archbishop's residence was ideally suited for Hamilton's purpose, because it was on the south side of the High Street at one of its narrowest points on the slope leading up to the Cross, which would force Moray to slow down as he rode past, thus allowing Hamilton to take aim and shoot him.

Hamilton went into every bit as much detail as in any modern political assassination and insisted on every possible precaution so that he should not be detected before he could carry out the murder. He had the front room in the Archbishop's home draped in black so that there was no chance of even his shadow revealing his presence and a matress was placed on the floor to muffle his footsteps. Outside the wooden balcony overlooking the High Street was hung with white linen sheets, which were a common sight in Linlithgow as they were manufactured in the town and often stretched out to bleach in the sun. This time however, one small hole was left with just enough room for the barrel of a gun.

Outside Hamilton's preparation were equally thorough. He obtained a good horse from the Abbot of Arbroath and once harnessed, tethered it at the back door of the Archbishop's house where he also ordered that the lintle be removed from the garden gate so that immediately he fired, he could make a dash for the rear entrance and ride off with no obstructions to hinder his flight. Obstacles such as a bale of hay were even placed in the lane leading in from the High Street to hamper any of Moray's servants or companions who might try to give chase.

Hamilton's wait in the Archbishop's House must have been a lengthy and tiring one because the Regent did not depart on January 22nd. Next morning Moray still did not appear and it was not until lunchtime that a sudden bustle in the High Street told Hamilton that the moment was near.

A minute later Moray emerged from his lodgings and joined his entourage for the ride back to Edinburgh. Completely unsuspecting the Regent spurred his horse to encourage it up the slope towards the Cross. At last Moray was within Hamilton's sights. The moment he had waited over two years for had arrived. He raised his heavy gun and fired, thus committing the first murder in Scotland ever carried out with a firearm.

"The murderer shot him with a lead bullet below the navel", recorded George Buchanan at the time, but evidence detailed by Patrick Cadell in his recently published book, "Sudden Slaughter", suggests that Moray was actually shot in the back and that the wound beside his navel was where the bullet came out after passing straight through his body. In any case Moray was so badly injured that he died that night, while Hamilton was already making good his escape to France, where he went on to make his career as a paid gun man, carrying our several other assasinations. The murder which he committed in Linlithgow is recorded on a plaque on the wall of the Sherriff Court House, which somewhat ironically now stands on the former site of the Archbishop's house.

Mary's son James VI did not pay his first visit to Linlithgow until 1579 when he was twelve and then he stayed for only one night. He paid another short visit in 1583, but his longest stay came two years later in 1585 when plague in Edinburgh forced the Royal Court to leave Holyrood.

Keeping to Scottish royal tradition James offered Linlithgow Palace as part of his dowry to his bride to be, Princess Anna of Denmark and in 1590 Danish Court officials arrived 'to tak' sasine'. James obviously aimed to impress the Danes because on the evening of 15th May one of the most magnificent banquets ever was staged in the Lyon Chamber.

Next year James travelled to Denmark to marry Anna and after a

The tower of the Town House is framed by the stone arch way of the Ooter Yett, the outermost gate, of Linlithgow Palace, which was erected by Mary Queen of Scots' father King James V in the 16th century.

The plaques on the wall trace the descent of our present Queen from Mary Queen of Scots, who was born in the Palace in December 1542.

dreadfully rough crossing of the North Sea, which the king blamed on witchcraft, he brought his young bride to Linlithgow as part of their honeymoon. Like the other Stewarts before him James VI seems to have been particularly fond of Linlithgow and ordered several improvements to be carried out to the outside of the royal suite of rooms on the west side of the inner courtyard, where his carved initials can be seen.

Three of James VI's Scottish parliaments were held in the great hall at Linlithgow during the plague of 1585 and again in 1593 and 1596. Later in 1596 on 18th December James returned to Linlithgow, not at all in a mood to join in the traditional Christmas celebrations, but in a very bad mood and a great fury. All of this unseasonal ill temper was provoked by happenings in Edinburgh the previous day when the Protestant ministers had dared to harangue James in the Tolbooth in Edinburgh about the king's alleged leniency to Scotland's Catholic lords and his lack of support for the reformed church. As someone who believed implicitly in the divine right of kings to govern as he alone pleased James was greatly indignant at the impertinence of the Presbyterian clergy and was even more upset when a great noise and commotion outside in the High Street turned out to be the local populace rioting in support of the ministers. Despite the danger James marched straight out of the Tolbooth and confronting the crowd is said to have warned them that he considered their behaviour treason and that he would punish the whole city of Edinburgh by leaving it, removing its law courts, ordering its buildings to be destroyed and even going so far as to sow its site with salt.

How much of this was bravado and how much real royal anger we shall never know, but at dawn next morning James put the first part of his threat into action by quitting Holyrood for Linlithgow. The thought that His Majesty might really close the law courts on which much of the city's prosperity depended sufficiently worried the magistrates that they turned on the ministers who had provoked the clash and the crowd and forced them to flee to England, while at the same time sending a messenger to Linlithgow to seek the King's pardon.

Three years later in 1599 it was the people of Linlithgow that James was chiding. For it appears from a letter which he sent to the magistrates that the inhabitants had been on the royal domain. In his letter James states,

'Provost and bailies of our burgh of Linlythgow we grete you weill. Forasmekill as we and our predecessors hes bein accustomat to have our horses watterit besyde our Paleice by the water yett in the Kirkgait by an ample passage swa that they mycht pace and repace by utheris without impediment. Nochtwtstanding being informit that sum inhabitantsis in that our burgh pretendand richt to the tenementis and ruids adjacent to our said loch has not only stoppit the passage of our said horsis by including the same by dyikis. Bot also in the late drouths of somer extendit the bounds and the limitis of thair tenementis far within owr said loch to the grait preiudice of our orchardis and yeardis adjacent to our said paleice by staying the samin to flow owr the auld boundis theiroft and causing the samyn in respect of your restreayning to owrflow owr Peill and ordhardis of our said Paleice geving us thairby to mervell of you, your slothfullness thairin and owrsicht in staying thame, which althogthir should have respectit us in that behalf. It is theirfor our will and we expresslie command you that upone the sicht heiroft ye stay all fardir building of the samyn dykis and destroy and cast downe all that ar allreddie biggit within the bounds of the flowing of our said loch except that dyik biggit by Nicholl Bell for restreayning of the passage frome our said Peill, as ye and ilk ane of you will answer to us upon your officeis and obedience and will discharge yourself theiroft, whairanent thir presentis sall be your warrand. Subscribit with out hand at our Castell of Sterling the 17th day of August 1599, sic subscib, James R.'

Like his predecessors, however, James usually liked to come to Linlithgow for relaxation and on one occasion wrote to the Duke of Hamilton at Kinneil House asking him to supply his best hounds and horses for a special hunt. This letter also makes interesting reading.

'Milorde, as I taulde ye at yours being with me, I ame sa contineuallie braggit with Milord Home that I have to defend the honour of Scotland at this tyme: he will be heir on Weddinsdaye next with nine couple of fleing fiends as they saye, theirfore I pray ye to send me with the bearare twa or three of your fleitest and fairest running houndes; and because in good faithe, I ame disproudit of horses I will in a hamelie manner praye ye to send me, lykewyse with the bearare, Griseld Blackstow, or if he be not in, in that case any other hunting horse and on my honestie na boddie shall ride on him but myself, and baith he and youre doggis shall be returned to you immediately. I command the guideman of Grange to helpe you to choose the doggis, thus not doubting ye will be a goodfellow in the aulde manner to this my reasonable request and with Goddis Grace, the English tykes shall be dung doun. I bid you fairweill, youre loving frinde in the aulde manner, James R.'

While James was eager on this occasion to 'dung doon' the English he was equally keen to accept the English crown in 1603. His departure for the court in London, the problems which he encountered there with the English parliament; and the difficulties and dangers which travel presented at the start of the seventeenth century meant that it was fourteen years before King Jamie paid his one and only return visit to Scotland. During all of this time, robbed of the royal attention which it had until then always enjoyed, Linlithgow Palace was obviously neglected. James received a letter from the Earl of Linlithgow reporting that the roof of the north quarter had fallen in and that the inner wall of the north facade of the courtyard had developed such an alarming list that it 'lukis euerie moment quhen the inner wall shall fall, and break your majestie's fontan.'

Nothing was done however until the king himself arrived on 30th June 1617. By this date Linlithgow not having had a royal visit for over a decade was in a state of great excitement. First there was the mystery of where many of the furnishings of the Palace had disappeared to and the embarrassment when the Privy Council ordered that 'diverse persons return "tapestrie, bedding and household stuff".' Amongst those named was no less a person than Lord Linlithgow himself who protested 'that he had little that belonged to the king' apart 'frae ane piece of tapestrie cuttit through by Andro Cockburn, foole. The tapestrie that was in Linlithgow was brocht oute of Stirling, quhen the laite Prince Henrie of famous memory, cam to Linlithgow, for hinging of his chalmer and that same tapestrie was sent fra Linlithgow to Holyroodhouse, to the laite Earl of Montrois, chancellor for the tyme. During the haill tyme that the Lady Elizabeth was at Linlithgow, her chalmir was nevir hung with the king's tapestrie.'

Despite such problems all was eventually ready for the king's coming and the whole population is said to have turned out to welcome James VI and 1st home to his Scottish kingdom, while Linlithgow not to be outdone by the other Scottish burghs had commissioned a special address of welcome. It was written by the poet William Drummond who at that time owned a house in Linlithgow and frequently stayed in the town and was delivered in a most unusual manner. For as the king entered the town through the High or East Port leading in from the road from

Edinburgh, he suddenly found himself confronted by an enormous plaster lion. Inside was concealed the local dominie, who appropriately bore the name of Wiseman. As James approached he proclaimed the poem which Drummond had prepared, bellowing out 'Thrice royal Sire, here I do you beseech
Who art a lion, to hear a lion's speech —
A miracle; for since the days of Aesop, No lion till these times his voice did raise up to such a Majesty; then king of men,
The king of beasts speaks to thee from his den,
Who, though he now enclosed be in plaster
When he was free, was Lithgow's wise schoolmaster.'

Although James only stayed at the Palace for one night it was long enough to convince him that work must be done to save the north wing and this was started the following spring on 2nd April 1618. On that day the king's Master of Works, James Murray employed a gang of men to start quarrying stones from Kincavill Quarry. By the end of April the supply of stone had been transported the two or so miles to the Palace and Master of Works Murray sought a meeting with the king's treasurer to arrange the employment of masons and wrights. William Wallace was appointed master mason and given a room within the Palace. At the end of February 1619 Murray applied to the Privy Council for permission to make alterations to the east and west quarters at the junctions between them and the new north quarter as this would enable him to arrange the doors and windows so that they matched the existing fabric. He did an excellent job for to this day the north facade is the most elaborate and pleasing in the courtyard with the pediments above the windows carved with the king's initials, Scottish thistles, roses for England, a harp, an angel and even a portcullis. By 1620 the work was almost finished and Murray asked permission from the Privy Council to order lead for the roof. In total the rebuilding of the north wing with its four floors of bedrooms each equipped with its own garde robe installed in the outer walls, cost the king almost £5000, an enormous sum in the seventeenth century.

Money was always a problem for James VI especially as the English parliament tried to attach so many conditions to the granting of it that one piece of news which James received from Linlithgow during his years at the court in London particularly excited him. It told of the discovery of silver in the Bathgate Hills to the south of Linlithgow and James immediately saw this as a possible solution to some of his financial woes.

The find was made in 1606 by a local coal miner, not while he was

Five turnpike stairs provided access to the upper floors of Linlithgow Palace. Four are situated at the corners of the courtyard, while the fifth was a later addition added to the middle of the north facade when it was restored by order of King James VI and I in 1620 to make it simpler to reach the many guest bedrooms situated in this block, which is worth exploring for evidence of its domestic details from its large open fireplaces where coal from Bonnytoun Pit was burned despite protests from the courtiers that the soot might damage their complexions, to the garderobes in the outer walls, where they perfected their toilets.

working under ground in his pit but by sheer chance when he was out enjoying a Sunday stroll. The miner, Sandy Maund was out walking alone on the hillside just above the Hilderston Burn when he idly kicked a large red coloured stone. As it bounced away down the hillside it broke open revealing dozens of tiny silver veins such as the old miner had never previously seen. Curious when he dug away the earth he found another stone which, when he smashed it open, sparkled in the sunshine.

Old Maund carried both stones home and the following Saturday night when he went down to Linlithgow for a drink, showed them to the other men in one of the inns. Among them may well have been some of Linlithgow's many hammermen or smiths who were used to working with metals because he was advised to take his finds all the way to Leadhills in Lanarkshire where the well known metallurgist, Sir Bevis Bulmer, was at that time prospecting for silver.

Despite the distance Maund took this advice and travelled on foot all the way to Leadhills where as soon as he saw the stones Sir Bevis identified the find as silver. Tests in the assay furnace soon proved that it was one of the richest finds ever made in Scotland. When word reached the king he at first granted a lease of all the mineral rights within the lands of Ballencrief, Bathgate, Drumcrosslie, Hilderston, Knock of Drumcross, Tartraven and Torphichen to his advocate in Scotland, Sir Thomas Hamilton of Monkland, but when in 1607 his majesty heard of the riches being found in the first of the mines, which was nicknamed 'God's Blessing' because it was such a bountiful horn of plenty, he promptly decided that he wanted a more personal involvement than simply the money from the lease. Consequently in December of that year Sir Bevis Bulmer presented a letter to the Scottish Privy Council from the king instructing him to arrange the shipment of 10 tons of stones from Hilderston, 'as weill the best as the worst sorte theirof' to London so that English experts might evaluate the Scottish silver. In this matter James well lived up to his nickname of the Wisest Fool in Christendom, because at the same time he also arranged for a similar ten tons of ore to be processed at Linlithgow's Silver Mill on the River Avon to make sure the English experts were reporting accurately.

The tests are said to have shown that every hundredweight of ore was producing the excellent result of 24 ounces of pure silver and with rumours that 'God's Blessing' was producing silver worth at least £100 a day, James promptly cancelled Hamilton's rights to the minerals and took them over as a royal monopoly. Hamilton received £5000 as compensation and the job of managing the mines along with Sir Bevis but after the original success production began to decline. The king blamed the Scottish miners, imported from the local coal pits, declaring that they were obviously too clumsy to work in the very narrow passages and confined spaces of the silver mines, some of whose workings were less than two feet or two thirds of a metre high, and gave orders to import miners from the lead and tin mines of Cornwall. When they failed to boost production, expert silver miners were summoned from Saxony in

Germany. They were shipped across the North Sea and landed at Berwick on Tweed from where they were rushed north to Linlithgow.

The local people viewed all of the miners and especially the newcomers from Germany with deep suspicion and demanded that the Provost appoint more Bailies to ensure the keeping of law and order lest the silver mine workers caused disturbances when they came down to drink on Saturday nights.

The miners had however little time to drink away their high wages because twenty four hour a day working was introduced to try to satisfy the king's demands for increased production. Two new shafts were sunk and these became known as the German East and the German West, but despite all of their efforts, production never recovered. The king therefore decided that denationalisation was the best policy and gave up his royal monopoly in favour of an international consortium made up of Sir William Alexander of Menstrie, of Nova Scotia fame, Edinburgh goldsmith Thomas Foulis and Portuguese businessman Paulo Pinto, who agreed to work the mines and pay the king a tenth of their profits.

The new consortium proved particularly unpopular in Linlithgow because to gain water for the new smelting plant they diverted water from the burgh mill. The Provost and magistrates protested to the Scottish Privy Council but got no satisfaction because of the king's support for the scheme.

Up in the Bathgate Hills too feelings were running high amongst the local landlords, who felt that it was most unfair that silver should be mined on their estates without them receiving any of the profits. Led by James Ross of Tartraven on 3rd September 1613, 'he with many accomplices came to the shaft of the mine and filled it full of stones and earth, so that the redding thereof held the workmen the whole day thairafter bussyed and excercised.'

No sooner had the miners cleared the mine than Ross and his angry neighbours returned on the night of 5th September and again filled in the shaft. Two days later Ross again returned this time supported not only by his neighbouring lairds but by all of their farmhands, 'armed with swordis, langstaffis and other weapons and having by menaces forced the workers to stop their labours, they filled the shaft with stones and earth.'

In the end, however, it was not the violence of Ross and his supporters or the more peaceful protests of the Linlithgow magistrates but the dearth of silver which resulted in the closure of all seven silver mines which had been sunk in the Bathgate Hills since operations started in

This old mill stone was uncovered at the site of Little Mill on the shores of the River Avon.
Avon is the old Celtic word for river and other local place names such as Mill Road and
Burgh Mills are a reminder of how many local mills its fast flowing waters once powered.

1607. From a production peak of over 200 tons of silver in the first year outpeak had dwindled to only a few tons by the time operations ceased around 1619 and although King James always retained the right to buy back his royal monopoly by paying Sir William Alexander of Menstrie and his colleagues £10,000 he did not take up the option and mining was not resumed before his death in 1625.

It was in fact over two hundred and fifty years later before another attempt was made to find silver in the Bathgate Hills by local colliery owner and mining engineer Mr. Henry Aitken. He secured mineral leases of the land at Hilderston and around Cairnpapple, the highest point in the Bathgate Hills, from the Earl of Hopetoun, from Mr. Andrew Gillon of Wallhouse near Torphichen and other local proprietors and started mining in 1870. He found not silver but nickel and marketed it at

£4. 13s. 0d. a ton. Nickel is a very poisonous substance and its discovery may help to explain the frequent reports by earlier seventeenth century visitors to the silver mines that both the children and the animals who stayed near the mine shafts always seemed sickly and ill. In 1873 several hens which had been pecking round amongst the piles of nickel ore were reported to have died.

Encouraged by finding nickel, Mr. Aitken sank a new and much deeper shaft to a depth of two hundred feet but he found neither more nickel nor any silver and this set back forced him to abandon the enterprise. Mr. Aitken continued to run successful coal and iron ore mines, but he always clung to the hope of striking silver and over twenty years later he came back to the hills to the south of Linlithgow to make one more final attempt. On this occasion he determined to re-open the very first of all the shafts, the old 'God's Blessing'. Rubble and stones blocked the shaft but once they were cleared the old workings were revealed still in good working order. Mr. Aitken's careful examination however showed that the first miners had worked well and that no silver remained. For another two years Mr. Aitken continued his quest for silver, but in the end in 1898 after spending several thousand pounds he finally, reluctantly gave in. Out of all the men who joined in this West Lothian treasure hunt it was therefore only the original owner of 'God's Blessing', Sir Thomas Hamilton who did well out of it. He became Earl of Haddington and by the time he died in 1637 had amassed one of the biggest fortunes which any Scot up until that time had ever possessed.

By that time King Charles I, the son of James VI and I had succeeded his father to the throne and in 1633 he made his one and only royal tour of Scotland. He was also the last monarch ever to live in Linlithgow Palace and his visit caused every bit as much commotion and excitement as that of his father back in 1617.

Linlithgow had been expecting a visit from the new king ever since the death of his father in 1625 and repairs including work on the King's Tower, the Queen's Tower, the south east tower and the Lyon's Chalmer had all been carried out. When at last, eight years later, Charles finally did decide to come north of the border the preparations still became hectic and as well as the lieges of Linlithgow involved many of the people in the surrounding countryside and villages.

An order was sent by the Scottish Privy Council to magistrates of Linlithgow to provide food for the king and all of his followers, including provisions for a banquet at the Palace. In addition the people of Linlithgow were 'forbade to slay, sell, buy or eat any kind of partridges, black cocks, earth hennes, termigants, capercailzies and muirefoullis' as all of these game birds would be required for the royal party. The townsfolk were also ordered to provide, 'clean handsome and neat lodgings for the King's attendance' and to make certain, 'that the bedding should be clean and well smelled'.

Outside, too, the magistrates decreed that Linlithgow must be spruced up for the royal visit. Orders were given for the repair of the grammar school, while Nicol Townis, owner of a thatched tenement which was said to be in an atrocious state of repair was ordered to slate the roof before the arrival of his majesty. All of the inhabitants were instructed to ensure that the rubbish in their middens was well screened from the royal view and that all filth was scraped from the streets. Even the beggars, who normally frequented Linlithgow, were ordered not to enter the burgh boundaries during the whole of the royal visit.

Up at the Palace a host of tradesmen including joiners and masons made last minute repairs and alterations. The royal apartments were replastered and freshly decorated while the intricately carved fountain in the inner courtyard was carefully cleaned.

Finally on the last day of June fresh reeds and matting were laid on the floors of all of the rooms to be used by the king and the royal party while the local bakers were summoned to the Palace to help bake extra supplies of bread and help the cooks prepare the pies for serving on the morrow.

Before daybreak next morning on 1st July 1633 over 600 horses and carts summoned from farms all over West Lothian from Livingston in the south to Bo'ness in the north assembled in the courtyard of Holyrood Palace ready to transport all of King Charles I's possessions on the first stage of his royal progress through Scotland from Edinburgh to Linlithgow. The king himself and his immediate household travelled in several very heavy and cumbersome royal carriages to allow the passage of which all the roads between the city and Linlithgow had to be repaired and widened. This work was placed in the charge of Tam Dalyell of the Binns. General Tam, an ancestor of Linlithgow's present member of parliament, had been one of the 'Hungry Scots', who had followed King Charles' father James VI to London eager to work for the wealth and positions which the Union made available for the first time. He had loyally served both monarchs and now, equally loyally, ensured that all of the local farmers carried out the repairs to the roads. But he was himself secretly disappointed because he had desperately hoped that his royal master would honour his home with a visit. The beautifully appointed royal bed chamber with its ornately decorated plaster ceiling can still be seen on the first floor of the Binns, but it remained unused because Charles preferred instead to return to the home of his Stewart fore-fathers at Linlithgow Palace.

The arrival of the royal cavalcade in Linlithgow caused great excitement as the king's coach entered through the High East Port from Edinburgh Road and drove along the crowded High Street. As it approached the Cross the two town drummers, both kitted out in new bright red uniforms, beat out a drum roll of welcome, before the royal procession proceeded on round through where the rose garden is now situated to catch its first view of the Palace.

And what a view it must have been with banners flying from the four watch towers afront the massively impressive east facade and the gold painted lion rampant on the huge coat of arms above the Old Entry gleaming proudly in the morning summer sun. Across the long wooden drawbridge the royal party must momentarily have been plunged into darkness as they passed through the double entry or yett before re-emerging into the light of the inner courtyard there to admire the new north wing, which Charles' father had commissioned but never seen.

With Linlithgow Palace at long last completed to perfection it was sad that this its last royal stay was but for one night. For after a night of feasting and revelry King Charles departed next morning on the next part of his royal journey to Stirling Castle and although it could not have been realised at the time, he became the last monarch ever to stay at the Palace. For great changes were soon to come with the civil war, the execution of the king, and the coming of the Commonwealth which was to change the life style of the whole country and that of Linlithgow with it.

CHAPTER SIX

Linlithgow for Leathers

AFTER the departure of King Charles I following his one night stay at the Palace, the next major excitement to occur in Linlithgow took place in 1646. In that year the dreaded plague broke out in Edinburgh and as it raged unchecked through the old city's overcrowded and very unhygienic tenement lands along the High Street it was decided to evacuate both the Scottish parliament and the university to the healthier country air of Linlithgow.

As on previous occasions when the parliament had met in Linlithgow its members soon established themselves in the Great Hall of the Palace, but the Lord Provost of Edinburgh and the city magistrates had to write to the Provost and councillors of Linlithgow for help in housing the university, its professors or regents as they were called and their students. The reason that this appeal came from the Lord Provost and magistrates was that at this time Edinburgh — unlike Scotland's other three universities in Aberdeen, Glasgow and St. Andrews — was a 'tounis college'.

Immediately the Linlithgow councillors received the letter from the city fathers asking them to supply, 'the college, regents and students with accommodation until the judgement be removed', they replied that 'they were weil pleasit to assist them and condescended to gie them fyne schoolis in the Kirk; dividit and made ready by themselves'.

The reason that the Provost and councillors were able to be so helpful was that by coincidence St. Michael's had just been gutted of the old higglety piggelty pews installed after the Reformation and was lying empty ready for the installation of new ones for which tons of timber had just been brought over Flints from Kinneil Woods near Bo'ness. So instead of pews the members of the Guild of Wrights quickly erected partitions between the huge stone pillars of St. Michael's lofty nave and installed wooden benches for the students. Within days word was sent to Edinburgh that all was ready to house the classes so that the students' studies would not be disrupted.

Very few of the students could afford to hire horses to ride the eighteen miles over the rolling Lothian countryside from the city to Linlithgow and so most made the journey on foot with their books and few other belongings bundled under their arms or tied in packs on their backs.

This sudden influx of students, professors and members of the Scottish parliament greatly worried the Linlithgow councillors, who feared that this big increase in the demand for lodgings might well tempt their fellow townsfolk to fleece the visitors. To prevent this, therefore, they issued the following order which read, 'It is ordainit that the following be observit by the haill inhabitants and no contravenit; viz., the price of the noblemen, chamber, cole and candle with two beds for twenty four hour, 20 shillings; and of gentlemen and Commissioners of Burghs, that space, thirteen shillings and four pence; and the price of the rest of the lodgers resorting to the said burgh for cole, candle and bed for twenty four hour, six shillings and 8 pence; and the grooms and footmen for their bed, 3 shillings'.

It does not however, appear that the Edinburgh students were allowed to occupy their beds over long, because they had to make their way along the High Street and up the steep, narrow cobbled Kirk Gate to St. Michael's shortly after dawn ready to start the first lectures at 6 a.m. Work continued until 9 o'clock when the students were allowed a one hour break for breakfast. At ten the church bells tolled to announce the resumption of classes, but when they rang again at noon the students knew that they were free for the remainder of the day.

How the Edinburgh students spent their leisure time in their new surroundings is unfortunately not recorded but the local inns no doubt welcomed the increased trade while others of the young men, some of whom were as young as fourteen and fifteen, perhaps enjoyed the new sport of golf and other healthier pursuits in the green acres of the Peel.

The Peel skirts the shores of Linlithgow Loch, so others of the students may have spent the afternoons fishing and boating, while a few may even have summoned up the energy to climb the nine hundred and eighty feet of Linlithgow's famous local landmark, Cockleroi, to stare back east to Edinburgh to wonder how the outbreak of the pox was progressing.

After several weeks the plague did abate and the professors deemed it safe to return but before doing so they expressed; 'their gratitude to the council for their great favour and courtesy', and presented them with, 'the haill deallis brought into the Kirk in making up the schoolis for the University, to be employed by them to such purpose as they shall consider most convenient'.

Now as Edinburgh University looks back and reflects on more than four hundred years of history, it is possibly worth a thought that it was in many ways a pity that the professors and their students hastened back to the city as soon as the sickness ended. For Linlithgow could have provided it with the kind of campus, which Edinburgh as a 'tounis college' unlike St. Andrews, Oxford and Cambridge sadly has never possessed.

Whatever was done with the timber with which the temporary university lecture rooms at Linlithgow were constructed it was definitely not used to make pews as had originally been intended for later church records show that their installation did not finally take place until 1672 and new wood had to be acquired for the purpose. One reason why the job was not completed upon the departure of the students in 1646 may well have been that the church authorities had other more pressing problems upon their minds as the congregation was being torn asunder by quarrels over support for the Solomn League and Covenant. Finally, as in many other places in Scotland in 1649, the congregation split into two factions called the Protesters (who were staunch Covenanters) and the Resolutioners.

Most of the common folk of the town supported the Protesters, but the Magistrates were in favour of the Resolutioners named after a resolution aimed at providing freedom from the strictures of the covenant and this inevitably led to trouble. The Protesters called upon the Rev. Alexander Guthrie to be minister at St. Michael's, but the magistrates refused to have 'this son of an Edinburgh tailor', as they described him, preaching the gospel to them.

The magistrates, therefore, ordered the Presbytery not to induct Mr. Guthrie to St. Michael's and went so far as to ban its members from entering the burgh. Furious at this interference the members of the Presbytery came instead to St. Magdalene's and were about to install Mr. Guthrie, when the Provost and magistrates arrived, 'fell upon them, wounded some of them and drave them by violence from the place.'

Despite their disarray the members of the Presbytery re-assembled shortly afterwards at Pardovan, the home of one of the Protesters, Walter

Stewart, and there inducted Mr. Guthrie to his new charge at St. Michael's. Not surprisingly Mr. Guthrie's ministry in Linlithgow was a very troubled one. Sadly, it was also a·very short one because just over two years later at the age of only 27, Mr. Guthrie died.

By this time St. Michael's had even more troubles to worry it because with the execution of King Charles I in 1649 and the arrival of the Commonwealth, Oliver Cromwell commandeered it as a storehouse for his army and a stable for his soldiers' horses. Cromwell's Roundheads even went so far as to use both inside and outside of the old church for musketry practice and the marks can still be seen along with those on the stones where they sharpened their swords. This damage was nothing however to that which they caused at Blackness Castle, where they blew up the massive battlements during the destruction of which local legend maintains the Devil appeared!

As far as the Provost and Magistrates of Linlithgow were concerned Cromwell himself was the Devil incarnate and when they heard that he was coming in person to occupy the Palace they departed in haste for Fife where they took up residence in Culross. Cromwell twice stayed at the Palace which he always referred to as Linlithgow Castle, a term recalling the fact that like that earlier English conqueror Edward I, he fortified it by building battlements all the way from either side of the archway at the top of the Kirk Gate through the Peel and down to the shores of the loch.

Meanwhile on the opposite shore of the Forth at Culross the Provost and Magistrates 'met and togther continued in love, enacting in so far as they were able for the weill of the puir toune and rightly governing of the commonwealth thereof and setting the same to the greatest avail that it could be put unto in so calamitous times.' In the end, however, they were forced to recognise that the 'calamitous times' had come to stay at least for the present and were forced to come home caps in hands to seek conciliation with the Commander in Chief, whom Cromwell had left in charge at the Palace. One of the first things they did was to plea for St. Michael's to be handed back for worship. The reply came from Cromwell's chief officer in Scotland, General Monk who demanded a guarantee of £5000 sterling, 'for their peaceable deportment, and not wronging, nor molesting the garrison.' They were also forced to stop their religious quarrel with the Protesters by agreeing to build a wall across the middle of the church. Thus St. Michael's was divided for the first time with the Protesters holding their services on one side of the wall in the chancel while the Provost and Magistrates along with their fellow

St. Michael 'had his wings clipped' it was said when the Lords of the Reformation stormed into Linlithgow and 'cleansed St. Michael's' at the height of the Protestant fever, but unlike the other statues which they smashed and swept from the kirk, he was so firmly built into the fabric of the church that he stubbornly resisted their efforts to remove him and so continues to this day as patron saint to look down from his vantage point on the passing scene in the Kirk Gate.

Resolutioners held their acts of worship in the nave. This meant that the Provost and Bailies had been greatly humbled as the nave was totally bare and unfurnished.

Meanwhile the townsfolk were getting on surprisingly well with the English soldiers who, apart from their temporary misuse of St. Michael's and their demolition of the original town house and other old buildings in the Kirk Gate to provide stone for their battlements, had not committed any of the dreadful deeds which the Provost and magistrates had dramatically predicted. Instead their presence is said to have been generally beneficial for the town because not only did they bring increased trade but they are also credited with having taught the leather workers of the Cordiners Guild better ways of tanning with the result that Linlithgow rose to become of equal importance with Perth as Scotland's principle leather making centres and at its height the Linlithgow leather industry boasted no fewer than seventeen tanneries, twelve skinners and eighteen currying works. In particular Linlithgow became famous for the production of footwear and again the credit goes to Cromwell's troops as it is claimed that they showed the local craftsmen how to make army boots. Thus Linlithgow's cobblers, or snabs, as they were always known locally, became famous and could be seen all along the High Street sitting at the doors of their workshops, wearing their long thick leather aprons or dadlies, and hammering away at their lasts using the millions of nails or tackits, which Linlithgow's tinkers were delighted to supply. Essayist Alexander Smith in 'Dreamthorp' describes the snabs 'in red night caps and leathern aprons', but does not mention that they were often teased by visiting Bo'nessians who are alleged to have chanted 'Linlithgow for Leather' and to have then very pointedly held their noses because of the pungent smell. The snabs, however, apparently always had the last word because local tradition has it that they always retorted 'Aye and Bo'ness for blethers'.

One reason for the Bo'nessians' patronage of the Linlithgow snabs is that they were far famed for their manufacture of leather, high sea boots which were specially treated with goose oil to make them water tight. These were much in demand by the Bo'ness sailors and especially the whalers who boasted that they never learned to swim as their Linlithgow boots were guaranteed to drown them in seconds should they ever be so unlucky as to fall into the icy Arctic Sea where any attempt to swim would only have prolonged the freezing agony.

Agony of another kind was often deliberately caused by the Linlithgow snabs as, long before Lochgelly specials ever terrorised Scottish school children, it was Linlithgow leathers which reigned supreme in many classrooms as several of the snabs specialised in producing tawse for teachers. While two Linlithgow shoe-making families still have shops in the High Street neither Morrison nor Stobie keep up the tradition of tawse production but it is interesting to note that the last school straps in Scotland are still carefully handmade by a cobbler in Edinburgh's St. Stephen Street.

Almost inevitably it appears that the Linlithgow snabs often used their long lithe tawse on their own apprentices. This these lads were forced to accept as it was legal for their masters to punish them including the use of corporal chastisement, but when a snab's bad tempered wife whipped one of them they quickly complained to the Deacons' Court.

It was the Deacons' Court which laid down all the rules for the apprentices. Usually it was stated that a boy must serve his master for five years during the first year of which his parents were expected to pay the master for the lads board, lodging and clothes. Thereafter the master provided the apprentice's keep but it was often written into their contract that at the end of the five years the apprentice would repay this by working for a further whole year without pay before he could himself start up in business as a fully-fledged, time served journeyman.

The Deacons' Court also laid down the standard which apprentices had to reach before they could become recognised tradesmen. But the court also looked after the apprentice's interest not only by safeguarding him from any too severe or unfair punishments as mentioned above but also by guaranteeing to find him another master should the original one die, go bankrupt, or otherwise go out of business during the five years that the lad was bound to him.

Apart from ensuring that all tradesmen in the town served proper apprenticeships, the Deacons' Court also prevented any unqualified outsiders from setting up businesses in Linlithgow and ensured that any craftsmen who did move to the town could produce proper indentures. Not only did the Deacons' Court check the standard of the workmen, they also regularly checked the standard of the work which they produced and decided on fair prices for the various goods. Also, on the money side, the Deacons regulated wages and the contributions which the craftsmen had to pay weekly into the common good fund maintained by each guild to ensure that it could look after its members and their families in time of need. This included paying sickness benefit to members off work ill and funeral benefits for both the member and his wife as a decent funeral was considered of very great importance.

The eight incorporated guilds in Linlithgow during Cromwell's time were the Baxters, Coopers, Cordiners, Fleshers, Smiths, Tailors, Weavers and Wrights. Other unincorporated crafts included the Carriers or Carters, Dyers, Horse Dealers, Meal Makers and Masons. They were generally considered to be of a lower class and until the end of the century were not eligible for election to the town council. Many of them were, however, obviously striving to be upwardly socially mobile — as it might be expressed nowadays. For instance, in 1647 the Carriers sought permission to create a common good fund like those run by the incorporated crafts and promised to pay in a levy on every horse load of goods which they carried to or from the town. It is interesting to note from this that goods were generally carried by horse, and not by road because of their still atrocious state, and that over 1500 loads were carried to and from Edinburgh in that first year.

Another example of members of an unincorporated trade seeking to become established came in 1660 when the Gardeners were officially recognised as a Benefit Society and by the end of the century the unincorporated Dyers were sufficiently well off to invest their surplus in a bond. It is interesting to note that it is the Dyers who, alone of all the old trades, remain active in their participation in riding the Marches.

At this time, apart from the Marches, four fairs were held in Linlithgow each year, on the Thursday after Pentecost, on 24th August which was always known as St. Magdalene's Fair; on the 21st September which was St. Matthew's Fair; and on 24th October. The most important and most popular was always the St. Magdalen's Fair.

In addition, regular weekly markets were a major feature of Linlithgow's town life.

While most of the stalls were grouped around the Cross and along Market Lane, some goods were always offered for sale in other parts of the town: meal was sold from a room below the classroom in the Burgh School where the Rose Garden is now situated! Timber was always sold at the West End where a timber yard still exists as most wood was brought over Flints from Bo'ness and this was therefore the nearest and most convenient site. West Port was also always the scene of the weekly horse markets which were held from January until May.

Until 1645 markets in Linlithgow were always held on Saturdays but in that year the Provost and magistrates decided that they should be moved to Fridays because all of the drinking and subsequent rioting which always seemed to occur on market nights was not deemed a proper prelude to the Sabbath day!

During the period of Oliver Cromwell's rule the moral code was particularly strictly enforced. The records of St. Michael's contain details of how after the Sunday service the elders were ordered to patrol the streets to ensure that no children were out playing and that families at home were reading their Bibles and learning the catechism. Even the celebration of Christmas, which had formerly been such an important event in Linlithgow, was forbidden.

St. Michael is kinde to straingers states the engraving below the angel and the coat of arms carved on the well erected in 1720, which still stands on the pavement in front of the ornate Victorian St. Michael's Hotel at the east end of the High Street. On the opposite side of the steep lane at the entrance to the hotel can be found another of Linlithgow's curiousities, the terraced house known as 'Hame's Best', but why it got this name or why it was painstakingly carved in the stone above the door is a mystery.

It is not surprising that when Oliver Cromwell died and his son failed to succeed him the people of Linlithgow were delighted to celebrate the restoration of the monarchy and the coming to the throne of King Charles II in 1660. To show their support the Town Council despatched a messenger to ride to Edinburgh to purchase the largest royal coat of arms which he could obtain. It was proudly erected in St. Michael's where it can still be seen, complete with its silver unicorn, Scotland's original royal heraldic beast, and its golden lion rampant; not above the royal pew as many visitors think but above the pew which the Provost and councillors still occupy when kirkin' of the council ceremonies take place. The royal pew in St. Michael's is incidentally at the foot of the pulpit steps at the start of the choir.

Festivities in Linlithgow were even greater the following May on the first anniversary of the restoration when, more certain that the new monarch was safe on the throne, bonfires were lit and the Covenant was publicly burned. Cruickshank in his 'History of the Church of Scotland' described the scene as follows.

'After publick service the streets were filled with bonfires on both sides of the streets, that it was not without hazard to be among them. The Magistrates about four o'clock in the afternoon went to the Earle of Linlithgow's lodging, inviting his lordship to honour them with his presence at the solemnity of the day. The Magistrates were Andrew Glen, provost, Robert Milne, Thomas Hart, George Bell, James Glen, baylies. The Earle of Linlithgow came with the Magistrats to the mercat place accompanied with many other gentlemen, where a table was covered with confections. They were met with the curate of the place, Ramsay (now Bishop of Dunkeld), who prayed and sang a psalm, then eating some of the confections they threw the rest among the people; the fountain all this time running with French wine of several colours and Spanish wine, and continued two or three hours. His Lordship, with the Magistrates and gentlemen drank the King and Queen's and all the Royal familie their healths, his Majesty's Commissioner the Earle of Middletoun, — breaking baskets of glasses. At the Mercat Cross was erected a crowne standing on an arch on four pillars. On the one side of the arch was placed a statue in the form of an old hag having the Covenant in her hands with this superscription, A GLORIOUS REFORMATION.'

Everyone however did not join in the rejoicing and the next few years saw Scotland torn asunder between those who supported the restoration of Episcopacy, as the king desired, and those who still wanted to remain loyal to the Covenant, with Linlithgow in the thick of the strife. At St. Michael's the minister, the Rev. Alexander Seton, brother of Sir Walter Seton of Northbank on the hillside between Linlithgow and Bo'ness found that although the partition between the chancel and the nave had been removed in 1661, his congregation was still divided between those who attended his services, conducted in the manner approved by king and parliament, and those who defiantly took to the Bathgate Hills to take part in the open air conventicles. Unlike many people at this time the Rev. Mr. Seton appears to have been very tolerant as he is quoted as saying, 'Poor people. Why should they be hindered in preaching and praying what they pleised?' For this he was roundly condemned by the authorities who accused him of 'encouraging the phanaticks to continue the conventicles.'

The job of ensuring that the conventicles ceased in the Bathgate Hills, or anywhere else in this area, fell to Tam Dalyell of the Binns, ancestor and namesake of the present Member of Parliament for Linlithgow. As far as Dalyell was concerned he was simply doing his duty as a loyal royalist in supporting the king by ensuring that the people worshipped in the official manner but the highly efficient manner in which he pursued the Covenanters made him the most hated man in Scotland.

'Bloody' Dalyell they nicknamed him and since then the historians have concentrated on this aspect of his career while neglecting his more praiseworthy qualities. Noteworthy amongst them was his undoubted loyalty to the monarchy which led him in 1649 to declare that he would neither cut his hair nor his beard until a king was restored to the throne. The huge comb with which he cared for his locks during the following eleven years of Cromwell's Commonwealth can still be seen amongst his relics at the Binns.

Dalyell himself however was unable to stay at the Binns during these eleven long years but was forced to go into exile. This he did by travelling to Russia where he used his prowess as a soldier to re-organise the Czar's army.

At last in 1660 the restoration of King Charles II enabled Dalyell to return home. Back at the Binns, which takes its name from the Gaelic Bein meaning hill, he devoted much of his time putting his estate into good order and was amongst the first in Scotland to practise landscaping, planting deciduous trees to form not only eye catching features but also shelter belts for his fields and cattle. As well as being an innovator on the land, the first Tam was also a noted man of letters and one contemporary visitor to the Binns remarked with awe that a ladder was required to reach the many books in the library which he established as a proud feature of his home.

No matter how efficient a farmer, how practised a soldier and how cultured a gentleman, however, it was Dalyell's campaign against the Covenanters which was to make him famous or infamous.

So successful was he against them that the Covenanters declared that he must have the Devil on his side. Water, they declared, boiled and bubbled in his huge leather riding boots while such a favoured son of the De'il was he that bullets simply bounced off his armour. Rumours spread of the atrocities which he was alleged to have committed from roasting Covenanters to death in the huge oven which can still be seen in the Binn's kitchen, to being first in Scotland to torture them with the thumbscrews to extract confessions. With a name like Dalyell the Covenanters even declared that Tam was the De'il's namesake.

Surprisingly the Covenanters admitted that Dalyell did occasionally quarrel with his hellish master and two of the most famous stories about the General concern such disputes. On one occasion the Devil is said to have been so angry with his protegé that he declared that he would blow down the House of Binns. 'Oh no you wont', Dalyell is said to have declared and promptly built the Binns turrets to pin the house down and they can still be seen to this day.

A frequent subject of dispute between Dalyell and the Devil was said to be their nightly games of cards and on one occasion when he lost the De'il is said to have been so furious that he heaved the great marble topped card table right out of the house. From then on it was never seen again until one hot summer day at the end of the last century when the famous Royal Scots Greys were watering their horses at the pool which borders the long drive up to the big house. The water level was unusually low because of the midsummer drought and suddenly the troopers saw a large object just below the surface. Two of the cavalry horses were harnessed to it and as they pulled what emerged from the dark waters of the pond than a marble topped gaming table which today enjoys a place of honour in the laigh hall of the old house.

The Binns is of course the home of the Royal Scots Greys, or Royal Scots Dragoon Guards as they are now known, because they were specially raised by General Tam as his secret weapon against the Covenanters.

Far too often he had been thwarted in his campaign to capture them when they had seen his Redcoats advancing across the green Scottish hillsides. Dalyell sent to the Netherlands for bales of grey Flanders cloth which he had made into the new uniforms from which his regiment derived its name, their famous grey chargers not coming upon the scene until much later in the regiment's proud history.

The Scots Greys proved as efficient as Dalyell had hoped and the Covenanters suffered several defeats culminating in the Battle of Rullion Green in the Pentland Hills, to the south of Edinburgh. This victory, however, also resulted in Dalyell's resignation because, strictly against his orders, women and children amongst the prisoners were slaughtered and as a man of honour he declared that he would have no more to do with the campaign.

One of the Covenanting characters who survived the slaughter and was brought to Linlithgow after Rullion Green was a Bo'nessian called Muckle Jock Gibb. Muckle Jock, who was lodged in the town gaol in the Kirk Gate, was a fundamentalist preacher. Big Jock had apparently as much charismatic charm as any of the current crop of American television evangelists, because he had established himself as the leader of a group of enthusiasts called The Sweet Singers so called because they sang psalms everywhere they went. All women, they fervently believed that Muckle Jock was a direct descendant of King Solomon and that all of his pronouncements were definitely true.

Jock's deliverances were many and varied, ranging from a prohibition of the use of any of the names of the days of the week because they were derived from those of the heathen Norse gods, to a pronouncement that the city of Edinburgh was such a den of vice and iniquity that it would be utterly destroyed by God. Jock also decreed that it was undoubtedly evil to pay any taxes to the government as all offerings must be made solely to the Lord. At first Dalyell and the authorities regarded Jock simply as an eccentric and when he was brought to Linlithgow he was ordered to be flogged and sent home to Bo'ness but although the burgh executioner no doubt laid on the lash extra hard given the chance to whip the back of a Bo'nessian, even this apparently failed to deter him. For Jock continued with his Covenanting campaign until his excesses forced the authorities to arrest him again and have him transported to the West Indies where his further exploits provided the basis for John Buchan's exciting book, 'Salute to Adventurers'.

Other prisoners lodged in Linlithgow during Covenanting times included all of those taken captive after the Battle of Bothwell Bridge. First mention of this event occurs in the minutes of St. Michael's Kirk Session where it is noted that: 'June 1679 there was no sermon in regard of His Majesties forces marching through the toun befoir Bothwel Bridge fiecht.'

'His Majesties forces' proved too much a match for the untrained Covenanting troops and around 1200 of them were taken prisoner. Their arrival in Linlithgow on their way to punishment in Edinburgh caused great scandal as many of them were naked. So perturbed at this shocking state of affairs was local dominie Alexander Kirkwood, master at the Grammar School that he went to the Captain of the Guards, Alexander Brown whom he persuaded to give him his regimental cane as a symbol of safe conduct to the soldiers. He later recorded in his own words the humanitarian deeds he then performed as follows. 'From Three in the morning until Ten in the forenoon, I alone stood on the

Flesh-market Wall, and gave in over it above 300 suits of cloaths, and exceeding much meat and drink, not without hazard to my person being often like to follow the cord with which I let down the barrels to the prisoners, of whom many thereafter came back and thanked me heartily for the favour I had done them.' Where the lowly paid dominie obtained all these goods to give away is not explained but he later used this incident in evidence of his unbiased nature in his famous and lengthy battle with the Provost and Magistrates which we will come to shortly.

Linlithgow's well known support for the royalist cause and the House of Stewart brought it another more willing visitor at this time in the shape of no less a dignity than the Duke of York, brother of Charles II, who himself later became James VII and II. The Provost and Magistrates were delighted once again to have a royal visitor in residence at the Palace and during his stay in 1681 made him a freeman of the burgh and laid on such a feast for him in the recently rebuilt Town House that it cost Linlithgow the then princely sum of £1856. 7. 6 Scots.

Another well known personality who frequently lodged in a house in the High Street at this time, again probably because of Linlithgow's royalist leanings, was Claverhouse, Lord Dundee, the famous Bonnie Dundee of Jacobite songs. When Linlithgow's erstwhile royal visitor James II succeeded Charles II to the throne, admitted his Catholic faith and, later, produced a Catholic heir, Dundee still loyally supported him despite the Bloodless Revolution of 1688 and a year later in 1689 gave his life for him at the Battle of Killiecrankie.

The coming of the Protestant William and Mary of Orange to the British throne completely altered the political as well as the religious scene in Linlithgow just as in other parts of Scotland and Rector Kirkwood thus found that although he had been appointed in 1675 to replace dominie David Skeoch dismissed for his Covenanting views and his attendance at conventicles he, in his turn, was now very much out of favour.

Despite the fact that he was one of the best known school masters in the country and that his famous 'Kirkwood's Latin Grammar' is said to have been used in every grammar school in Scotland, Kirkwood to his fury found himself commanded to appear before the Provost and town councillors whom, in the long battle of words which followed, he sarcastically dubbed the Twenty Seven Gods of Linlithgow. To make matters worse for Kirkwood the Provost at the time was young Walter Stewart of Pardovan whom he described as a mere lad scarcely out of the schoolroom. Now from the heights of his position as Provost, Stewart

This 18th century engraving by J. H. Le Keux depicts the east and south facades of the inner courtyard of the Palace and shows how damaged the famous fountain erected by King James V became during the years after the fire which destroyed the royal residence in 1746. It was restored in Victorian times and will be turned on several occasions during 600th anniversary year including during the seven performances of the son et Lumiere pageant, which will be amongst the highlights of the celebration festivities in September.

demanded that Kirkwood attend Protestant services. Kirkwood refused. He was promptly dismissed as master at the Grammar School and thrown out of the dominie's house along with his Dutch wife, Goletine van Beest, and all their fine Dutch furniture.

Kirkwood promptly went to court. The legal wranglings went on for years but eventually in 1712 the proceedings reached the Privy Council where the lords found in his favour. Linlithgow had to pay him damages and costly expenses. Thus was vindicated the freedom of the dominie whose former pupils included John Earl of Stair who boarded with Kirkwood and Colonel James Gardiner of Burnfoot near Carriden, who features in Sir Walter Scott's Waverley Novels.

In Kirkwood's time Linlithgow Grammar School was indeed one of the most famous schools in Scotland and employed three masters in addition to the rector, a considerable teaching force in those days. Emphasis was on the teaching of Latin, although it is said that the pupils preferred to use Kirkwood's grammar books to squash the big black beetles which scurried down their desks. Another ploy in which the grammar school boys are said to have delighted was rushing out of the classroom at breaks in their lessons on wet days to see if the rain had washed down any skulls from the graveyard at St. Michael's which rose above their playground and then using them to play primitive games of football.

Girls did not attend the Grammar School but were instead either educated privately at home or attended the dame schools several of which were held by women in rooms in their homes in the High Street. There they learned the alphabet, how to read simple texts from horn books and how to sew.

After his dismissal from his post in Linlithgow and while he fought the Twenty Seven Gods in the courts, Kirkwood became master of the grammar school in Kelso where he proved an equally controversial figure. Instead of becoming secretary to the local Kirk Session he became secretary at the Border town's episcopalian meeting house. Thus out of favour from the outset, Kirkwood soon found himself in trouble with the Session who publicly reprimanded him when he refused to strap several of his pupils reported to him for misbehaving in church at the Sunday service. No doubt encouraged by the knowledge that misdeeds committed in the pews on Sunday would not, unlike under their previous dominie, mean the tawse on Monday morning, the boys were even worse behaved during the sermon on the following Sabbath. Furious the Kirk Session again publicly ordered Kirkwood to fulfill his expected role as master of the Grammar School by suitably chastising the culprits. Again he refused and later got his own back on the Session, for daring to interfere with the way in which he ruled his scholars, by attending one of their meetings and loudly criticising all the local burgesses whom they proposed making elders!

When they heard of Kirkwood's subsequent rows in Kelso, the Provost and councillors in Linlithgow may well have considered themselves lucky only to have read about themselves in the satirical pamphlet 'The Twenty Seven Gods', rather than having to suffer a personal tongue lashing such as he inflicted in the Borders town.

CHAPTER SEVEN

Jacobites . . . and Trade

DESPITE the foolish and in the end very unprofitable litigation with Rector Kirkwood, Linlithgow at the end of the seventeenth and beginning of the eighteenth century appears on the whole to have been a town well run by its twenty seven councillors. They were made up of the Provost, four Bailies, the Dean of Guild who was responsible for trading affairs, the Treasurer, twelve councillors and eight deacons of the incorporated trades. The eight deacons were elected annually by their guilds and were not eligible for service as magistrates. The other nineteen members of the council were elected again annually at the meeting of the council nearest to Michaelmas, with usually only three or four changes in their number. They then chose the Provost from amongst their number, while the existing Bailies decided who should be Bailies for the following year. All these arrangements were then submitted for approval at a meeting in the Town House of all of the burgesses of the town, but this was usually simply a formality. The council sent a representative to the Convention of Royal Burghs and chose Linlithgow's M.P. Town Council meetings were held regularly at 8 o'clock every Friday morning. Typical business on the agenda included road repairs, water supply, sanitation, rules for trade and matters to do with the market and those in other neighbouring towns from which Linlithgow claimed dues.

These dues together with the customs levied in the market provided the funds to lay the High Street from West Port to Low Port with cobbles or setts or causies as they were known locally. Only the centre of the High Street was covered with these rounded stones, leaving the sides or loanings as they were described for the parking of carts a privilege still jealously guarded to this day as a unique area of parking with which neither police nor parking wardens can interfere. Where the loanings were at their broadest the Dyers were also allowed to erect their drying poles and stretch out their cloth which must have added vivid splashes of colour to the High Street scene.

An equally vivid picture of Linlithgow's prosperous textile industry at this time was painted in words by no less a writer than the author of 'Robinson Crusoe' Daniel Defoe, when he visited the town at the start of the eighteenth century. Officially Defoe was in Scotland to write a journal of his travels, but it was whispered that he was really in the pay of the English government and was spying for them in preparation for the campaign leading up to the Act of Union of the Parliaments, which was passed shortly afterwards in 1707. In Linlithgow, however, Defoe stuck strictly to writing about the local commercial scene which he described as follows: 'At Lithgow there is a very great Linnen Manufacture, as there is at Glasgow; and the water of the Lough or Lake here, is esteem'd with the best in Scotland for bleaching or whitening of linnen cloth: so that a great deal of linnen made in other parts of the country, is brought here either to be bleach'd or whiten'd.

The people look here as if they were busy, and had something to do; whereas in most towns we pass'd through they seemed as if they look'd disconsolate for want of employment. The whole Green, fronting the Lough or Lake, was covered with linnen-cloth, it being the bleaching season and I believe a thousand women and children, and not less, tending and managing the bleaching business.'

Defoe sums up by writing, 'Lithgow is a pleasnt, handsome, well built town.' Much of this was undoubtedly due to the constant vigilance of the local councillors who were always on the alert for the appearance of any 'dung heaps, middens or whin stacks' which they deemed illegal within sight, or possibly smell, of the High Street.

Whin stacks were considered particularly dangerous as a possible cause of fire which was a dreaded danger because many of the poorer houses still had thatched roofs. Each householder was ordered to provide his home with a ladder high enough to reach the top of the roof and each burgess also had to provide the town with a leather fire bucket. It is interesting to note that the entrance to the town's earliest fire station in the ground floor of the Town House can still be made out at the foot of the Kirk Gate, but no date is recorded as to when the appliance stored there was first used or whether it was hand or horse drawn. The fire station later moved round to the other side of the Cross where the frontage of the Coffee Neuk still bears reminders of its former use.

Congestion and traffic at the Cross led in the 1970s to the removal yet again of the fire station to its present modern premises with their distinctive tower in Philip Avenue at the West Port. Another interesting link with past efforts to protect properties in the town from the dangers of fire is the small Sun Fire Insurance plaque which can still be seen on the front of Number 79, High Street, opposite the Cross, which showed that its proprietor had paid his dues and that the brigade should attend and deal with any outbreak.

From fire to water Linlithgow's Town Council was equally diligent and at the start of the eighteenth century there was a Scottish saying 'Glasgow for bells, Linlithgow for wells' referring to the many wells which were, and in some cases still are, features of the High Street. Furthest east was the Whitten Fountain which stood in front of the Star and Garter Hotel, where the roundabout is now situated and which took its name from John C. Whitten, a former Sheriff Clerk of Midlothian, who died in 1889 and left £1,700 to Linlithgow with the request that a wrought iron fountain be erected on the site of a former well and that trees be planted along the south side and at the east end of the High Street. Today he is still remembered in the town through the place name Whitten Lane, although his trees and fountain have long since sadly been removed. Coming east the next well bearing Linlithgow's famous motto 'St. Michael is kinde to strangers' can still be seen, in front of the much later Victorian built St. Michael's Hotel. St. Michael's Well also bears Linlithgow's other coat of arms depicting the saint. Linlithgow is indeed believed to be the only town in Scotland with two official coats of arms.

The main well in the town was always the Cross Well. By far the most elaborate of the wells with its three levels the Cross Well's carved figures are believed to represent people from the town's past including the town drummer. In 1633 to mark the coming of King Charles I it was surmounted by a carved unicorn. The Cross Well has always been the place where crowds have gathered on Hogmanay to welcome the New Year and during the celebrations in the first few minutes of 1988 the old unicorn was unfortunately toppled by one of the town's more enthusiastic young men. Vandalism of a more deliberate kind has also robbed the Black Bitch carved on the front of the Cross Well of its head, but now fortunately restoration at a cost of over £5000 is promised so that the old well can once again occupy its rightful place at the heart of the town.

For those who did not want to walk to the Cross for their supplies of fresh water there were three other wells between it and West Port; Lion Well, Dog Well and, the last to be erected, the New Well. The remains of

The Cross Well has always been the heart of Linlithgow and is still the accepted gathering place for many local people to bring in the New Year. At New Year 1987 some of the young revellers clambered to the top of the three tiered fountain and accidently toppled the unicorn from its pinacle. Now however the unicorn, Scotland's original heraldic beast which can also be seen carved in the Queen's oratory in the Palace, has been restored to its pride of place atop the well in time for this year's 600th anniversary celebrations and royal visit. The present well was erected in 1806 and all of the elaborate carvings including the statues of the town drummer and his accompanying flute player were the work of Edinburgh stone mason Robert Gray. The intricacy of the stone work is all the more remarkable as Gray had lost a hand fighting in the Napoleonic Wars and carried out all of the carvings with a chisel in his good hand and a mallet attached to the stump of his arm.

the latter can still be seen but all traces of the other two apart from their place names have disappeared leaving us to ponder that they probably took their interesting names from the carved masks of a lion and a dog from whose mouth and snout their waters possibly poured.

One of the early Linlithgow Town Councils greatest feats was in arranging piped water supplies to all of the wells and as one of the first towns in Scotland with such a supply this as much as the burgh's healthy country air already mentioned, may have been responsible for Linlithgow's record of freedom from infectious diseases. Examples of the early waterpipes used to bring supplies to the Palace can be seen in the Palace museum and presumably those used to feed the wells in the High Street were similar.

As well as ensuring fresh water for all of the lieges, Linlithgow Town Council also insisted on high standards of hygiene with, as already mentioned, no middens or dung heaps in the High Street. Although just as today the local council had no jurisdiction over Linlithgow Loch, which still has its own separate Royal Police Force, the Town Council of old did act to protect its waters from pollution as it was used as a source of water not only by the tanneries but by the bakers and brewers.

Another effort which the Town Council made to keep Linlithgow healthy was to insist on quarantine regulations during time of plague in Edinburgh or any of the surrounding towns and anyone who had visited an infected area had to remain outside the burgh boundaries for a week or else remain confined to their own home for a similar period with the door barred and bolted by the Bailies. Such precautions appear to have worked well because few outbreaks of plague were ever recorded in the town, and any which did occur were very minor.

Linlithgow's main danger from infection, of course, came from the foreign shipping which docked at its out port of Blackness or at its much hated rival at Bo'ness. At Blackness at least, as it was within Linlithgow's official bounds, the Town Council could at least take steps to ensure that its rules were enforced, but as the three miles which separate the town from its harbour was considered too great a distance to allow the Bailies to administer it effectively a separate magistrate was always appointed. As his position was not strictly official he was always referred to as the Baron Bailie and was expected each year on Marches Day to report and account for his actions to his fellow Bailies of Linlithgow as the present occupant of the post, Mr. Robert Fleming, still does faithfully right down to the present day.

While making his annual speech and ensuring that all is in order for

New Well was one of several which lined the High Street and, in the days before piped water, supplied local homes.

Marches Day in Blackness are now the sole duties of the Baron Bailie such was very definitely not always the case. In the seventeenth and eighteenth centuries he was a very important and powerful figure charged with ensuring all duties due to Linlithgow were collected and that the port was conducted in a safe and orderly fashion. The Baron Bailie had the right to levy fines and to flog any sailors or other persons who became involved in fights.

The main exports through Blackness were heavy cargoes of coal, salt, rough woollen cloth, skins and hides. Corn, oats and wheat were sometimes exports and sometimes imports depending on the harvest. More important than its exports, however, were its rich imports. Some cargoes were made up entirely of wine while others were mixed. An inventory of these reads like that of a treasure store including parcels of Chinese silks brought to Holland by the sailing ships of the Dutch East India Company and re-exported, velvets from the Netherlands themselves, tapestries and arrass cloths from Flanders, fine Dutch linens, damasks and cambrics. Foods, too, featured prominently amongst the imports landed at Blackness including such delights for prosperous Scottish palates fed up with potatoes and oatmeal as spices, pepper, nutmeg, cinnamon, mace and cloves, plums, damsons, figs and raisins, almonds, capers, olives, peas and beans.

As these imports were all light in weight the ships docking at Blackness usually also carried cargoes of heavier materials to act as ballast and keep them stable as they crossed the often stormy North Sea and these often consisted of iron, decorative blue and white Delft tiles for fireplaces and the red pantiles which can still be seen on the roofs of many buildings in towns in the area and in a few places in Linlithgow itself.

Baltic timber for building was also imported through Blackness but its availability depended on the harvest on Scottish farms as most of the supply came from Norway and that country insisted that all ships exporting wood had first to bring in cargoes of grain. Thus a poor Scottish harvest also meant a dearth of building timber the following spring.

One of the most interesting cargoes to be shipped through Blackness was tobacco. This trade which grew greatly in importance after the Union of the Parliaments in 1707, meant that England could no longer exclude Scottish merchants and their ships trading with her colonies as had until then been the case under the much hated English Navigation Acts. These restrictive measures had insisted that all goods from the English colonies such as Virginia had either to be carried in English

Red pantiles, grey stone gables and crow step gables were all features of No. 270 High Street, long since demolished to make way for the featureless concrete blocks of flats which sadly disfigure the centre of the town.

merchant vessels, thus ensuring a ready supply of ships for the English navy in time of war, or in vessels of their colony of origin which were few and far between and that all of the cargoes no matter for where they were destined had first to be landed at an English port.

Scotland had tried to fight back by establishing her own rival colonies under the ill fated Darien Scheme and two of its ships are believed to have been provisioned at Blackness but it was the inclusion of Scotland under the former English laws after 1707 which finally let Blackness benefit from the new tobacco trade. As the Navigation Acts still insisted that all cargoes from the now British colonies had to be first landed in this country the tobacco was brought to the Clyde and imported at Port Glasgow by the Glasgow merchants. There it weas carefully loaded into panniers and placed on the backs of horses to be carried right across the narrow waist of Central Scotland to Blackness where it was stored in the old Guildry until a ship might arrive to re-export it to the cigar making experts in Amsterdam. The prosperous Blackness tobacco trade lasted for approximately half a century. The first blow to it came in 1776 when their success in the American War of Independence meant that the thirteen former American colonies no longer had to obey the Navigation Laws about sending all of their produce to Britain and so tobacco could go from these former mainland colonies direct to Holland. The second blow came towards the end of the eighteenth century with the completion of the Forth and Clyde Canal making it far simpler to ship most of what remained of the tobacco cargoes by barge direct from Bowling to Grangemouth. The third and final blow was an act passed by the government which for customs duty and excise purposes limited the number of British ports which could handle tobacco and excluded Blackness from the list.

During the short heyday of the Blackness tobacco trade one family who were prominent in it were the Mitchells of Glasgow. They began not only to import and export the raw tobacco leaves but also to manufacture them and to this day some of this famous firm's products still bear the Black Bitch of Linlithgow as their trade mark.

Another story linking the Mitchells with Linlithgow is that typical of Victorian times the family wished to use some of their profits for the public good by establishing a library. The only condition attached was that it be known as the Mitchell Library but so the story goes the Linlithgow Councillors could not agree and so the largest library in Europe is situated at Charing Cross in Glasgow giving the city yet another claim to being Europe's 'City of Culture'.

Back in the middle of the eighteenth century it was of course from Europe that Prince Charles Edward Stuart launched the Jacobites last ill fated attempt to regain the British throne but as in other parts of the south of Scotland he received far less than the overwhelmingly enthusiastic welcome which he might have hoped for when he arrived in formerly royalist Linlithgow, because few of the Royal and Ancient Burgh's merchants relished a fight which might disrupt the ever increasing trade which they were at last beginning to enjoy as a rich fruit of the Union.

It was on the morning of Sunday 15th September 1745 that the Bonnie Prince reached Linlithgow. Most of the population were devoutly making their way to church at St. Michael's when the word spread that the Prince's army of Highland clansmen had reached West Port. As they began their march along the High Street the would be worshippers ran back down the Kirk Gate to catch a first glimpse of Prince Charles Edward. On being informed that the bells were ringing out for Protestant worship rather than to welcome him back to the town where his Stewart forebears had had their Royal Palace, the Prince is said charitably to have sent a message up to St. Michael's to the minister the Rev. Robert Dalgleish urging him to go on with his service but without a congregation no sermon was preached that day.

While St. Michael's was deserted the Palace was crowded as Linlithgow's leading Jacobites rushed to join with Mrs. Glen Gordon who led the celebrations to welcome the Prince. Noticeable by his absence, however, was Provost John Bucknay who although known to be a Jacobite sympathiser obviously felt that for a man in his leading position discretion was the better part of valour and rode off for Edinburgh. For the other Jacobites, however, the festivities proved memorable with the fountain in the Palace courtyard flowing for the last time with wine and the Prince at his most gracious especially towards the ladies. They included Provost Bucknay's wife and daughters who wore tartan gowns complete with Jacobite white cockades and when the Prince took his leave he paused at the Cross Well to kiss their hands.

While the Jacobites of Linlithgow were sorry to see Bonnie Prince Charlie depart the rest of the townsfolk were not at all sorry to see the back of his Highland supporters who stole and plundered their way along the High Street, taking whatever took their fancy as was their wont and as they almost considered their right. Possibly because he knew their habits Prince Charles ordered the officers to move the men out to St. Magdalene's where they camped for several hours before moving on east to spend the night in the fields near Three-Mile-Town on the way to Winchburgh. The Prince himself spent the night at Kingscavill House but, despite all of the loyal toasts earlier in the day in the Palace courtyard, very few of the burgesses from Linlithgow chose to follow him.

Such was the case in the rest of the country and so after reaching Derby the Jacobites retreated. As they did so the government dragoons under their commander, General Hawley prepared to intercept them and orders were sent from Edinburgh to Linlithgow to provide provisions to feed these troops. Word of this was leaked to the Jacobites who on January 13th 1746 under Lord George Murray staged a raid on the town in the hope of seizing the supplies. As the Highlanders searched the town their sentries reported government dragoons approaching along the road from Bridgend. Murray ordered his cavalry to ride out through the High East Port and head them off while he rounded up the rest of the clansmen and beat a hasty retreat, but by the time they reached Linlithgow Bridge it is said that the two armies were within shouting distance of each other. A second Battle of Linlithgow Bridge did not however, take place as contact appears to have been limited to hurled abuse as the government officer in charge, Major General Huske, had only half of the Hanoverian troops with him and decided not to risk a fight.

Instead he ordered his men to camp for the night at Linlithgow Bridge. Next morning they were joined by the rest of the Redcoats and marched on to Falkirk while their Commander in Chief, Hawley, remained in Linlithgow and spent the night at the Palace. Next day he travelled on to Falkirk to catch up with his men who were camped at Bantaskine. The following morning he accepted an invitation to breakfast with Lady Kilmarnock at Callendar House and was completely taken by surprise when the Jacobites launched an attack. The second Battle of Falkirk thus turned into a sudden and very unexpected defeat for the government forces and Hawley was forced to order a humiliating retreat to Linlithgow where along with his troops he occupied the Palace.

During the next fortnight the disgraced Hawley was replaced as Commander in Chief by the famous 'Butcher', the much hated Duke of Cumberland who was renowned for his callous cruelty. He arrived in Linlithgow on 31st January 1746 bringing reinforcements from Edinburgh for the government troops which increased the strength of the army encamped in Linlithgow that cold winter night to over ten thousand. At the Palace the Redcoat officers celebrated the arrival of their new commander and the revenge for the Battle of Falkirk which he promised would soon be theirs. Carousing went on late into the night and Mrs. Glen Gordon who, despite her Jacobite sympathies was still also in residence as keeper of the Palace, is said to have remonstrated angrily with Cumberland, Hawley and the other officers, about the huge fires which they had lit in every fireplace in the Palace and especially about the enormous bonfire which they had allowed the soldiers to build to keep themselves warm beside the fountain in the courtyard.

Her protests were laughed at but Mrs. Gordon had the last word when she declared, 'Aweel, Aweel, I can rin fra fire as fast as ony General in the King's army', alluding sarcastically to General Cope's defeat at Prestonpans and more recently to Hawley's retreat from the Jacobites at Falkirk. Sadly, however, Mrs. Gordon's sarcastic taunt turned to reality the

View of Linlithgow. St Michael's Church with its golden crown of thorns and the ancient ruins of the Royal Palace dominate the Linlithgow scene as viewed over the roof tops of the buildings which crowd one of the steep wynds running down to the High Street.

Led by Linlithgow's well known Town Crier, John Watson, Linlithgow's Provost and visiting dignitaries walk round the Cross on Marches Morning. The Town House and the white-harled 18th-century Cross House, which is a fine example of Scottish vernacular building, provide an impressive background to the colourful scene.

Members of the Linlithgow Players present a masked drama in the Forecourt of the Palace as a part of the town's annual festival week, which features many similar lively performances.

Medieval craft fairs enliven the scene at the Cross on several summer Sunday afternoons each year. The fairs are well supported by local shopkeepers and traders, who join in the fun by dressing in appropriate costumes.

Jousting on the Peel provided an interesting spectacle in the Royal Park at a recent Linlithgow Festival Week.

St. Magdalene Distillery. The distinctive pagoda towers of the disused St. Magdalene's Distillery are being carefully preserved as this impressive stone building is sympathetically converted into luxury homes.

Loch at Sunset. Sunset in the west reflected in the still waters of Linlithgow Loch gilds this famous local beauty spot.

This view of the old houses at 372 High Street was taken shortly before they were demolished.

following morning when Cumberland and Hawley ordered their men to depart in such haste that they either negligently or deliberately failed to put out all of the fires and the fabric of the old Palace caught alight. As a result of all the straw and other bedding which the Redcoats had left scattered throughout the Palace the blaze spread swiftly and disastrously throughout the whole building.

With such a huge conflagration the townsfolk probably had no chance of succeeding in putting it out, although there is also a suggestion that they did not try as hard as they might because when word of the blaze was brought to Provost Bucknay, with his Jacobite sympathies, he is said to have replied, 'Weil, weil, those who kindled the fire had better extinguish it!'

Smoke was still rising from the ruins of the Palace the following morning as the townsfolk made their way up the Kirk Gate to Sunday worship at St. Michael's and it is said that sporadic outbreaks occurred for days thereafter. The rest of the country, or at least the people of Edinburgh, first heard of the disastrous blaze which had gutted the royal Palace of the House of Stewart in the Monday February 1st issue of the 'Caledonian Mercury' which carried a brief report reading, 'On Saturday, by some unlucky accident, the fine palace of Linlithgow was burnt to the ground; and we hear that the magistrates of Linlithgow have examined several witnesses in order to get knowledge of the true cause how that misfortune happened.' A few days later the January edition of Scotland's oldest periodic publication, 'The Scots Magazine', which appeared at the beginning of February carried a hastily inserted addition to its Edinburgh news column stating, 'P.S. — The ancient palace of Linlithgow was accidentally burned to the ground on 1st February. Soldiers were quartered in it the night before, and it was found that they had not been careful of their fires.'

At this period also it appears that St. Michael's Church was in a pretty ruinous state. In 1672 the church had once again been divided in two by a wall built across the chancel arch, the nave to the west being used for worship, while the chancel and choir to the east were used for burials. In the middle of the eighteenth century an army officer, Captain Burt, wrote, 'There is nothing remarkable in my way to Glasgow, but the church of Linlithgow — a noble Gothic building, now much in ruins, chiefly from the usual rage which attends Reformation. It is really provoking to see how the populace have broke and defaced the statues and other ornaments under the notion of their being relics of popery. As this town was our waiting place, a gentleman, the son of a celebrated

Scottish Bishop, who was with me, proposed that while dinner was getting ready we should go and see the inside of the structure, and as we took notice that great part of the floor was broken up, and that the pews were immoderately dusty, the precentor or clerk who attended us took occasion to say he did not apprehend that cleanliness was essential to devotion, upon which my friend turned hastily upon him and said angrily, "What, this church was never intended for your slovenly worship".'

Whether or not the worship in St. Michael's at this time was 'slovenly' it must certainly have been crowded, because in addition to the ground floor being full of pews five galleries or lofts were erected, supported by the pillars of the nave. A description of the church at this time reads, 'The pulpit is placed on the south side at the pillar nearly opposite the south door. The ground floor is occupied by nineteen pews with their faces to the east, twenty six pews with their faces to the south and ten pews with their faces to the west. There are five lofts. The gallery along the north aisle makes three lofts known as the North Lofts, the front seats of which are allocated to the King, the Earl of Linlithgow, and the magistrates of the burgh. On the right hand side of the pulpit is the East Loft, the half of which is assigned to the Guildry. The West Loft at the left hand side of the pulpit is allocated to the incorporations of smiths, tailors and cordiners.'

In 1768 St. Michael's was damaged by a severe late winter gale the weather cock being blown down and the steeple itself being damaged in the storm. The weather cock was of particular interest as it had been erected as long ago as the reign of King James III. It took the form of a mother hen with her brood of chickens together with the monarch's favourite motto, 'Ever watchful', and was so famous at the time that the Town Council ordered that it must be replaced on top of the stone crown which was then very much St. Michael's crowning glory.

Another repair which the council ordered and agreed to pay for was the restoration of one of the church's three bells. On 23rd January 1773 the councillors requested the Burgh Treasurer, 'to take the dimensions of the second bell in the church steeple, which has been fractured for many years and to consult with the proper persons at Edinburgh as to the expense of a new bell of the same dimensions and what allowance will be given for the old metal.'

At the next meeting on 6th February, the Treasurer reported that there was no-one in the whole of Edinburgh who could cast such a large bell and so the councillors instructed that, 'the second bell be taken down from the kirk steeple and carried to Borrowstounness, there to be weighed and put under the care of Mr. Charles Addison until the Provost write a letter to Mr. Lester, bell-founder at the Three Bells, Whitechapel, London, who they are informed is the properest person for furnishing a new bell, there being none in Edinburgh sufficiently versant in these matters.'

Less than a month later on 2nd March the Provost was pleased to inform the council that, 'he had written to London and received an answer which was read.' It was then ordered that, 'the old bell be immediately sent to London, and that the old stock along with it, in order that a new stock with iron and wheel may be there fitted to the new bell, which it is resolved shall be fixed and rung by a wheel.' It was also agreed that, 'the town arms and the year of God be put on the new bell and the Provost to correspond with the bell-maker on this subject.'

By May 15th the Provost was able to produce, 'a letter from Messrs. Peck and Chapman, bell-founders in London, signifying that in consequence of the order sent them, they had cast a new bell, which they had shipped on board the "Samuel and Jean" of Bo'ness, James Drummond Master, whose receipt dated the fifth current, is prefixed to the letter along with which there is also an account of the whole expense, amounting to £55. 3. 6 sterling and after deduction for the old bell metal of £27. 13. 1, the balance due turned out £27. 10. 5, which sum the Council authorise and empower the Provost to receive from the Treasurer in order to remit to London and appoint the accompt to be ingrossed.'

Thus the new St. Michael, replacing the original bell dated 1484, joined Ave Maria and Meg Duncan in the steeple high above Linlithgow and has been rung ever since. There are several customs relating to Linlithgow's bells. In time honoured fashion the first two St. Michael and St. Mary are always rung first to summon the congregation to the morning service leaving little Meg Duncan to ring out last and all alone. This is because the wee bell is said to take her name from the old woman who lived at the bottom of the Kirk Gate and who always scolded late comers as they scurried up the steep hill to reach their pews before the first psalm and it is said that the little bell's tongue is to this day every bit as sharp as the old wife's ever was.

At St. Michael's all three bells are also rung again at the end of worship. This old custom dates from the times when the richer members of the congregation rode to church with their families in their carriages. While they attended the service the coachmen took the horses to water them and no doubt their own throats at the coaching inns such as the Red Lion and Star and Garter in the High Street and at the end of the minister's sermon the beadle always rang the bells to warn them that it was time to return to take their masters and mistresses home for Sunday lunch. Today cars have replaced carriages and coaches outside St. Michael's but the custom of ringing out the bells at the end of the service still takes place.

On Marches day, too, Linlithgow's bells ring out including the bell in the steeple of the Town House and there is also a custom about this which says that the bells should ring from the time the Town House clock chimes eleven until the procession disappears over the brow of the hill at the Horse Market Head at West Port and then again when the procession appears back again from Linlithgow Bridge. Thus although the old saying, already quoted, 'Glasgow for Bells, Linlithgow for Wells' may have been true, Linlithgow still attaches a great deal of affection to its old bells and the people of the town were never happier than in 1945 when the bells could be rung again after their almost six years of silence during the period of the Second World War, when the ringing of the bells was reserved for the German invasion of our shores, which happily never came.

A more welcome visitor to Linlithgow away back in 1787 was Scotland's national poet Robert Burns who, even in his own time, was very much a celebrity. Burns was very well entertained in the upstairs room of the Golden Cross where he attended a meeting of the local Masons and became a member of the Linlithgow Lodge. The pediment of the Golden Cross, depicting the coat of arms of one time burgh Dean of Guild James Crawfurd can still be seen incorporated in the frontage of the flats on the west side of the Cross as a reminder of where Burns received Linlithgow's hospitality. No amount of hospitality, however, could persuade Burns to give a favourable write up to St. Michael's, where his eye alighted on the infamous 'cutty stool', or punishment stool, on one similar to which he had bitter memories of being humiliated in his church in Ayrshire. He wrote, 'St. Michael's is a pretty good old Gothic church; the famous stool of repentance in the old Romish way, in a lofty situation. What a poor pimping business is a Presbyterian palace of worship — dirty, narrow and squalid, stuck in a corner of old popish grandeur such as Linlithgow.'

A few years later in 1803 another lady with poetic connections Miss Dorothy Wordsworth was equally critical writing, 'The shell of a small ancient church is standing, into which are crammed wooden pews, galleries and pulpit — very ugly and discordant with the exterior.'

Many people in Linlithgow shared this unfavourable view and as early as 1775 the minister at St. Michael's wrote, 'The inside of this church at present does by no means correspond to its outward appearance. The east part might be converted onto an elegant place of worship and would, it is believed, accommodate as many as at present. This or some improvement of a similar kind will, it is hoped, be soon made.'

It was not however until 1812 that the next restoration of the church was begun. Four years earlier the people of the town had been startled to learn that the roof of St. Michael's was about to collapse. This news was contained in a report which read, 'The large beams immediately under the inside of the roof of the church were very insufficiently secured, and the ends of some of these beams, which had been originally inserted in the wall of the church have become rotten and decayed.'

The Provost and Councillors summoned the local wrights who as joiners agreed, 'that the beams appeared to them to be insufficiently secured and to threaten danger.' The Provost therefore consulted an Edinburgh architect, Mr. Alexander Laing whose report made even worse reading. 'Any repair that can be made on that crazy roof,' wrote Mr. Laing, 'will be attended with risk and danger. What is much needed is a new roof.'

The Council agreed, but the question of how much the various townsfolk were to pay towards the cost took four years to resolve. In 1812 a public meeting of all of the heritors of the town was called and chaired by Colonel Ferrier of Belsyde, which agreed that while the roof of the nave should be replaced, the space beneath should in future be used only as a meeting hall and that the actual church should be housed within the chancel, transepts and apse. Thus at one meeting two of St. Michael's greatest glories, its age old oak roof like the upturned hull of a great timber man o' war such as 'The Great Michael' and its magnificent carved stone chancel arch were condemned to destruction. The reason why the ancient chancel arch had also to be condemned, unlike the previous occasions on which the church had been divided, was that this time the meeting concluded that the church at the east end of St. Michael's fine building must be able to accommodate between 1,200 and 1,300 of a congregation and the only way to seat so many people was to incorporate with the chancel, transepts and apse, a bay to the west running back as far as the first pillars in the nave, which was to contain pews on the ground floor and more pews in a gallery on first floor level.

Ex-Provost and Councillor Sir Alexander Seton protested that these decisions were, 'irregular and illegal' but the work went ahead even although some people clearly recognised what terrible acts of sacrilege they were. They included future Provost, Adam Dawson of Bonnytoun

For over two hundred years the Star and Garter has welcomed visitors entering the town by the High East Port and the Low Port. Originally built as a coaching inn, it was also well placed to benefit from the coming of the railway station, which can be glimpsed behind its Georgian frontage.

House, who was present in St. Michael's the day on which the old partition was hauled down, before work on smashing the chancel arch and building the new one in line between the most easterly of the lippars in the Nave began. He described the scene as follows, 'We saw this edifice when all the obstructions were removed from end to end, and there stood St. Michael's in all its simple grandeur. The eye, ranging over a clear space of upwards of sixty yards, was met at the eastern extremity by three noble windows, altogether forming a spectacle unequalled, in our opinion, by anything that we have seen at home or abroad. Alas'. that such architectural excellence should ever be sacrificed for a system of utilitarianism, opposed so frequently, to every principle of taste.'

The newly restored church at the east end of St. Michael's was opened on Christmas Sunday 1813, but only seven years later a worse crisis was to hit the old church. For in 1820 rumours swept the town that the tower of St. Michael's was about to collapse. The Provost and Councillors summoned the towns tradesmen and asked for their views. After climbing to the top and examining the whole structure they reported back that, 'the spire is altogether in a very dilapidated state, being much rent in many places and that two of the spire arches which support the crown are in the worst possible condition and in the most dangerous state and cannot, to all appearance, stand for any length of time.'

Even more worried, the Provost and Councillors sought the advice of civil engineer Mr. H. Baird who wrote, 'The great weight of the top part has, by the arches pressing so heavily against the angles of the tower, rent it for a considerable way down. This has given the arches liberty to subside and caused several fractures in them and threatens the ruin of the whole spire.'

Finally the Town Council took advice from an Edinburgh architect Mr. Burns, who told them that he, 'found the walls to be so much injured by the lateral pressure of the flying buttresses which support the crown, on top of the tower that no time should be lost in either supporting this superstructure or removing it altogether. The flying buttresses on the south-east angle in particular, is in a most precarious situation, so much so, that if the pressure outwards was even to extend to a quarter or half an inch beyond what it is now, I have not the least doubt that the whole would fall to the ground.'

Various suggestions including cast iron corsets were put forward to try to save the old imperial crown, which seemed so much to signify Linlithgow's long links with Scotland's kings and queens, but after a year long debate it was reluctantly decided that it must be demolished to save the tower. Thus in the summer of 1821 the crown was removed.

St. Michael's remained without its crown for over a century and a half. Local people and visitors used often to reflect sadly on its loss, but it was not until the Rev. Dr. David Steel, father of the famous former leader of the Liberal Party and, later, himself Moderator of the Church of Scotland came home from St. Andrews, Nairobi, in Kenya, to be minister at St. Michael's that he decided that St. Michael's crowning glory must be restored. Dr. Steel had however very definite ideas about the new crown which should be erected. It should not he felt try to imitate the craftsman-ship of the stone masons of old, but should reflect all that was good and innovative about the craftsmanship of the Scotland of the 1960s. The new crown for St. Michael's was therefore constructed from prelaminated timber from the world's leading experts on this new fabric, Muirheads of Grangemouth, and it was clad in specially treated aluminium so that it will never lose its golden shine. There was great excitement when St. Michael's new Crown of Thorns representing the crown worn by Jesus at his crucifixion was finally erected and the controversy which it created has never ceased.

Without doubt St. Michael's golden crown has put both church and town very much on the map as the best known landmark in central Scotland, familiar to all travellers by rail between Edinburgh and Glasgow, and Stirling and the north, and to all drivers on the M9 motorway. Seen at certain times of the day with the sun striking on its golden finish it has an undoubted beauty, especially when seen from afar from the heights of the Bathgate Hills above the town, or from the west, entering the town past Avontoun Park. Seen close up, however, it still looks to many people as though unfinished. Twenty years later, 'When are they going to take down the scaffolding?' is a question still heard and 'The Misguided Space Missile' is one of the milder descriptions given to it. Other comments range from, 'Completely out of place on one of Scotland's finest medieval buildings' to 'The finest piece of 20th century architecture in Scotland'. How future generations will see St. Michael's new crown, time alone will tell.

CHAPTER EIGHT

Barging into Town

DURING the years of the Napoleonic Wars there were suggestions that Linlithgow Palace should be converted to house the overflow of French prisoners from Edinburgh Castle, but Lord Blair, President of the Court of Session in Edinburgh had recently bought Avontoun estate and it is claimed that he managed to dissuade the authorities and the prisoners were housed instead in old mill buildings at Penicuik. The Palace was, however, garrisoned for a short time during the early nineteenth century when the Irish navvies digging the Union Canal through Linlithgow caused so much trouble with their drinking and rowdiness when they came into the town to spend their wages in the inns and other hostelries along the High Street that the local inhabitants demanded protection.

Worried also about the effects of the canal were the local farmers who feared that their fields would be flooded.

The Union Canal was one of the last canals to be constructed in Britain, digging beginning in 1818 and being completed four years later in 1822. Originally it was planned to utilise Linlithgow Loch as part of the canal in a similar way to that in which Loch Ness was incorporated into the Caledonian Canal, but engineer James Baird managed to persuade the Union Canal Company that it would be much more efficient to build it as a contour canal on exactly the same level for the whole of its thirty one and a half miles between Edinburgh and Falkirk, thus avoiding time consuming locks with the exception of those linking it with the Forth and Clyde Canal at Port Downie near Camelon and thus substantially cutting costs.

At Linlithgow the Union Canal, therefore, followed a course along the hillside behind the town. During the construction of the canal its designer

James Baird lived at Canal House, beside Manse Basin and the window from which he paid the navvies on Saturdays can still be seen. They were nicknamed navvies as an abbreviation for navigationals or those who navigated the canal across the countryside. Two of Edinburgh's most infamous characters, the notorious body snatchers Burke and Hare, worked on the Union Canal and they both lived in Linlithgow while they helped dig the local section of it. It is interesting to note that two of the heavy iron mortsafes placed over newly dug graves for three weeks after burials in order to thwart the much feared body snatchers, who could only sell freshly interred corpses to the professors and students of Edinburgh University's school of medicine, can still be seen in the graveyard at St. Michael's.

There were however no body snatching incidents reported during Burke and Hare's stay in Linlithgow. The worst incident which was reported occurred as the navvies dug the canal to the west of the town where they cut through the pipes carrying Linlithgow's water supply, thus leaving the town high and dry for several days, possibly, it has been suggested, as a reprisal for the hostility which they had experienced from the local people who had been shocked by the rough, uncouth behaviour of the mainly Irish contingent.

Main reason for building the Union Canal was to provide the cheapest possible means of transporting coal from the pits of Lanarkshire to the homes of the ever growing city of Edinburgh. As the canal barges provided an excellent method of moving heavy cargoes compared with the still atrocious Scottish roads, quarries also grew up along the banks of the Union such as the one near Kettilstoun Mains, to provide stone for the building of the many new houses in Edinburgh's New Town as well as kerb stones for the roads which fronted them. The city's busy streets were at this period filled with horse drawn carts and carriages and the large amounts of resultant manure were loaded onto the empty coal barges at Port Hopetoun and Port Hamilton near where the Cannon Cinema now stands on Lothian Road and shipped out for sale as fertiliser to the farmers along the route of the canal including those around Linlithgow who thus benefitted from the Union instead of being damaged by it as they had at first feared.

Linlithgow also benefitted in other ways from the coming of the canal from the provision of an excellent supply of water for local industries such as St. Magdalene's Distillery to providing the town with a new regular and very reliable transport system. For in its day the Union was the fastest and by far the most comfortable route for passengers travelling

St. Magdalene's Distillery drew its water supply from the Union Canal. Sadly it is no longer in production and the few remaining bottles of its malt which it produced as well as supplying whisky for blending are now treasured possessions in many Linlithgow homes. The pointed pepper pot tops of its malt barns can be seen rising above the mass of the old stone building which is to be converted into luxury flats. At one time Linlithgow had four other distilleries and St. Magdalene's was built to compete with them by Mr. Sebastian Henderson.

between Edinburgh and Glasgow with express barges calling at Linlithgow several times each day. Fresh horses every eight miles, changed at stables such as those which can still be seen at Woodcockdale on the main road to Armadale, ensured that the passenger barges completed the whole 64 mile journey between the two cities in a smooth eight hours compared with a bumpy, dusty twelve on the swiftest stage coach. Those barges which carried the Royal Mail were also accompanied by a scarlet coated outrider who rode ahead of them blowing his bugle to warn any small boys and dogs to get off the tow path which ran the full length of the northside of the Union.

The passenger barges which provided Linlithgow with its links with the cities and neighbouring towns such as Philpstoun, Winchburgh and Broxburn to the east and Polmont, Laurieston and Falkirk to the west, were all excellently equipped for the comfort of their passengers. To ensure that the journey passed as quickly and as pleasantly as possible their facilities included bars and dining saloons while some even offered a small library of the latest novels to while away the time. For those who preferred livelier entertainment all carried musicians like the fiddler, Blind Tam, who played music for dancing on the open deck, as long as they were provided with plenty of pennies between tunes in the same way as the bands on the old Clyde steamers.

Aboard the barges passengers were offered the choice of two classes of travel, steerage in the stern, from which it took its name, and cabin, which allowed those who could afford it the extra pleasure of sharing the skipper's stories as the barge cruised right across Scotland. Highlight of the voyages for those in both classes was always sailing across the huge aqueducts such as the Avon Aqueduct to the west of Linlithgow which was a considerable feat of nineteenth century engineering designed by the country's most famous canal engineer Thomas Telford.

For busy merchants and other businessmen who considered that they could not spare a whole day for the inter city journey the Union Canal even offered an express overnight service. Sailing from Port Hopetoun in Edinburgh and Port Dundas in Glasgow each night at ten o'clock the night expresses arrived in the other city at six the following morning, in plenty of time for a whole day's business to be transacted. The 'Hoolets' or wee owls as the night express barges were affectionately nicknamed because of the big lights in their bows, were also very popular with honeymooners who liked to spend the first nights of their marriages in this romantic fashion speeding through the countryside at all of eight knots. To ensure that they could maintain this fast schedule the 'Hoolets' like the other passenger barges were equipped with sharp blades in their bows with which they could slash through the ropes of slower cargo vessels which failed to get out of their way in time. This was seldom necessary as the Union was excellently constructed thirty five feet wide along its entire length and five and a half feet deep, these facts together with its contour construction leading it to being nicknamed Scotland's Mathematical River.

An interesting description of the Union is provided by Alexander Smith in 'Dreamthorp', where he wrote, 'Every now and then a horse comes staggering along the tow-ing path, trailing a sleepy barge filled with merchandise. A quiet indolent life these bargemen lead in the summer days. One lies stretched at his length on the sun-heated plank; his comrade sits smoking in the little dog-hutch which I suppose he calls a cabin. Silently they come and go; silently the wooden bridge lifts to let them through. The horse stops at the bridge-house for a drink, and there

I like to talk a little with the men. They serve instead of a newspaper and retail with great willingness the news they have picked up in their progress from town to town. I am told they sometimes marvel who the old gentleman is who accosts them from beneath the huge umbrella in the sun and that they think him either very wise or very foolish. Not in the least unnatural! We are great friends I believe — evidence of which they occasionally exhibit by requesting me to disburse a trifle for drink money. This canal is a great haunt of mine of an evening. The water hardly invites one to bathe in it, and a delicate stomach might suspect the flavour of the eels caught therein; yet to my thinking it is not in the least destitute of beauty. A barge trailing up through it in the sunset is a pretty sight; and the heavenly crimsons and purples sleep quite lovingly upon its glossy ripples. Nor does the evening star disdain it, for as I walk along I see it mirrored therein as clearly as 'in the waters of the Mediterranean itself.'

It's interesting to wonder whether the bargees spent their drink money in what became known as the 'Pop Inn' an establishment which is said to have formerly existed on the northside of the Manse Basin which took its name from the fact that it had swing doors at both east and west ends so that the men could pop in at one, down a pint and pop out of the other in ample time to catch their horse pulling the barge. Although Alexander Smith describes the barge horse as 'staggering', the canal vessels were actually comparatively easy for the beasts to pull as once started there was no friction and loads were thus much easier to haul than on land. The marks of the ropes connecting the horses with the barges can still be seen gouged in the stone sides of the bridge to the east of the Manse Basin. Each of the bridges bears its number carved into its stonework, starting from Edinburgh and progressing towards Falkirk. Near Polmont, the Laughing Crying Bridge is particularly interesting. Carved on its east side and looking back towards Edinburgh and the work already done is a laughing face, while on the west side is a crying face looking towards the hard job which lay ahead of digging Scotland's only canal tunnel to carry it through the hills to Falkirk and its joining with the Forth and Clyde Canal at Port Downie near Camelon. Other interesting finds which can also be made along the tow path are the milestones which record mileage from Edinburgh on the east faces and distances from Falkirk on the other side and the section stones which marked the completion of each length of canal by the contractor who had submitted the lowest tender just in the same way as motorways are paid for nowadays.

Long before the coming of the motorways, however, it was the coming

The massive stone built viaduct was a considerable feat of engineering skill when it was erected at the beginning of the 1840's to carry the main railway line between Edinburgh and Glasgow over the valley of the River Avon near Linlithgow Bridge.

of the railway to Linlithgow on February 21st 1842 which robbed the Union Canal of its prosperous passenger traffic. For just as the canal had been faster than the old stage coaches, the railway now slashed the journey time between Edinburgh and Glasgow to two and a half hours with four trains in each direction every day. Cargo traffic on the canal continued throughout Victorian times but this century it declined steadily until in 1964 the Union was officially closed to navigation and proclaimed by the British Waterways Board to be a Remainders Waterway.

At this period the tide of time really seemed to have run out for the old Union and West Lothian County Council and other neighbouring local authorities sadly were allowed to fill in sections of it, and culvert it at various points, including Preston Road in Linlithgow, to allow roads to pass over it. Almost immediately local people began to realise what a terrible mistake had been made and while the unthinking demanded that the canal be filled in to safeguard children from falling into its waters, those who appreciated the local environment realised what a very valuable community asset was being destroyed.

First through SIWA, the Scottish Inland Waterways Association and then through the locally founded LUCS, the Linlithgow Union Canal Association, Linlithgow's new found canal enthusiasts banded together to convince the authorities of their error in not developing, far less simply preserving the canal. Today, LUCS, led by enthusiasts including regional councillor Mel Gray, Graham and Madelaine Harvey, Bob and Di Wild, Colin Galloway, Barbara Braithwaite, Danny Callaghan, Ian Raven, Liz Park and current chairwoman Ann Wigley is one of the liveliest of Linlithgow's many organisations. Its activities range from running Scotland's only canal museum in the original canalside buildings to operating a whole fleet of small craft from rowing boats through outboard motor launches to a pedallo and cabin cruisers which are ideal for family weekends exploring the quiet backwaters of the canal. Pride and joy of the LUCS fleet is, however, the replica nineteenth century steam pacquet 'Victoria' with which the society operates daily cruises throughout the summer season from Easter until September catering for school parties on weekdays and for members and the general public at weekends. Soon with a grant of money from the European Economic Community, LUCS hopes to remove the culvert which causes a barrier at Preston Road and replace it with a bridge, as was there in the past, thus opening up another eight miles of cruising waterway including the mighty Avon Aqueduct with its magnificent breathtaking views down into Caribber Glen and the valley of the River Avon below. Caribber Glen was formerly a very popular site for Victorian Sunday School summer outings by horse drawn barge and the opening up of the canal to the west of Linlithgow past Williamscraig will again make such treats a possibility. Other enjoyable outings already arranged by LUCS range from canalside barbecues to leisurely supper parties on 'Victoria'.

Highlight of each summer season on the Union is now always the highly popular Drambuie Rally which is organised by LUCS and during which teams from all over Britain race in inflatable dinghies. The event always draws crowds to Manse Basin and other vantage points along the canal's route through Linlithgow and it is particularly appropriate that the makers of Scotland's most famous liqueur have chosen to sponsor this event as the competing craft all pass Williamscraig, the former home of the MacKinnon family where, for many years, they kept the secret recipe for Drambuie as entrusted to them by Bonnie Prince Charlie before he departed Scotland's shores for the last time in 1746 and which is still used to produce the top selling drink at the family's distillery at nearby Kirkliston.

As well as LUCS and its supporters, several other organisations are now beginning to appreciate the many and varied possibilities for leisure which the Union Canal offers as a linear park. The Countryside Commission has appointed a ranger to amongst other things lead tow path walks which are particularly rich in interest for naturalists as the fact that unlike on road side verges, pesticides have never been used means that the canal banks are rich with wild flowers.

West Lothian County History and Amenity Society also organises canalside walks to study the industrial archaeology of the Union. More active interests also flourish from the young canoeists of the Linlithgow Canoe Club, who have their headquarters at Manse Basin to model power boat enthusiasts for whom the canal provides ideal calm waters and from joggers to walkers on the tow path.

In the nineteenth century Linlithgow also had a very important financial interest in the Union because the Town Council succeeded in insisting that every barge which passed through must pay a toll, just as coaches and carriages entering the town had to do at amongst other places the old toll house which can still be seen at Burghmuir, thus ensuring a welcome income for the town. When the loads formerly carried by the barges transferred to the new railway in the 1840s the Town Council immediately demanded that the Edinburgh and Glasgow Railway Company pay similar dues but it refused. The Town Council went to court but after years of costly litigation the case went to the House of Lords who found against the town. This was a severe blow for Linlithgow and, financially, it took the town many years to recover.

The coming of the railway also raised hopes that Linlithgow could profit from it in another way by becoming one of the inland holiday resorts, which were so popular during Victorian times thanks to the Queen and Prince Albert favouring Scotland for their holidays. Like places such as Bridge of Allan, Dunblane, Crieff, and Strathpeffer there was talk of Linlithgow with its beautiful loch and its famous wells becoming a spa town to which people would come to take the waters with the added advantage that salt water sea bathing could be offered at nearby Blackness.

St. Michael's Hotel and the Palace Hotel, whose premises on the opposite side of the High Street can still be seen with the proud name still visible on the facade, were erected at the east end of the High Street immediately convenient for passengers alighting at the new railway station. A little steam paddle pleasure launch, the 'Leisure Hour Steamer' was introduced on the loch by Charles Carlow and Garvie Davie's stables offered horses for riding and horse drawn landau to convey the visitors on tours of the surrounding countryside and down to the delights of the seaside at Blackness. But while Blackness enjoyed a brief revival in its fortunes with the building of holiday homes around the shores of the

E

Looking west along the Union Canal whose towing path runs on its north bank throughout the entire length of the town. The canal is rich in wildlife from the swans and ducks which frequent its waters to the wild flowers which grow along its banks.

West Bay, they were mainly used for weekend breaks by Falkirk businessmen and Linlithgow failed to reach the potential which it seemed to offer as a holiday town. This may have been because it was simply too close to Edinburgh to offer an alternative residential holiday centre. This is still a factor which is a problem for the recently formed Forth Valley Tourist Association which, a century later, is trying once again to boost Linlithgow's prospects as a holiday town. However, with more accommodation ranging from the new excellently equipped outdoor centre at Lowport to the new caravan park in the Bathgate Hills at Beecraigs Country Park, hopefully, it may succeed and thus obtain for Linlithgow a share in Scotland's fastest growing industry, tourism.

Back in the nineteenth century disappointed in its hopes of becoming an important holiday town, Linlithgow was pleased to welcome new industry in the form of the paper mills set up on the shores of the Avon. The rushing waters of the river had for long powered a series of mills and now the water power was utilised by the paper makers at Lochmill and nearby Avonmill both of which produced high quality paper from imported esparto grass including that on which the famous glossy London Illustrated News was printed for many years.

The earlier of the two works was Lochmill, which was already a going concern when it was acquired in 1855 by Mr. Thomas Chalmers who soon greatly enlarged it. Lochmill occupied the site of a much earlier meal mill which originally belonged to the Barony of Carriden near Bo'ness. By the time of the Reformation it was in the hands of the Burgh of Linlithgow and in the eighteenth century was operated by James Glen of Longcroft House. By the beginning of the nineteenth century it had ceased to function and for a time a printfield operated on the site.

It was under Mr. Chalmers that Lochmill really flourished and it was here during the 1890s that the production of imitation art paper by the waterfinish process was perfected. Demand for this top quality paper was met by the installation of one of the largest paper making machines in the country with a net width of eighty eight inches compared with the standard fifty five inches. The Chalmers family were always innovators and later Lochmill was one of the first mills in the world to take advantage of nuclear physics by installing a device which, by means of radio-active isotopes, controlled the thickness of the paper produced to any desired weight. Latterly, Lochmill was taken over by the well known Inveresk Group, which also still owns the papermill further up the Avon at the village of Westfield. It was subsequently closed as part of the Inveresk Group's reorganisation of its paper making interests.

Lochmill's near neighbour Avonmill belonged to Linlithgow's other well known paper making family the Lovells. The Lovells opened Avonmill during the 1870s like Lochmill, on the site of a previous printfield and utilised the dam on the Avon built by the printfield company to power the water wheel to drive the paper-making equipment. The Lovells always aimed to produce the finest quality writing paper from esparto grass imported from North Africa and built up a very high reputation. Their writing paper sold well and by exporting large quantities they managed to keep their men in work throughout the depressions of the 1920s and 1930s. Unfortunately their export business was devastated by the Second World War and after 1945 the foreign countries which it had formerly supplied began to make their own paper. In 1960 in a bid to remain viable Avonmill ceased cooking its own esparto grass and instead imported bulk prepared pulp again from North Africa. This helped to economise on fuel, but the savings were not sufficient to save the mill and it finally closed in 1971.

Both the Lovells and the Chalmers families prided themselves in their excellent relations with their workers and the latter are still particularly

The Union Canal provides Linlithgow was a peaceful quiet backwater where local residents can escape from the bustle of everyday life.

remembered for the Chalmers Hall which still serves the people of Linlithgow Bridge as a community centre.

On the subject of halls the 1840s saw a disastrous blaze partially destroy the Town House originally built in the Italian style in 1668 by the king's master mason John Mylne to replace that pulled down by Cromwell's soldiers. The fire broke out in 1847 and it was rebuilt the following year still with its arched piazza on the ground floor, but this time made in wrought iron as a result of the Industrial Revolution. It remained until 1907 when it was finally replaced by the now familiar double stairway, designed by Mr. W. M. Scott. The original tapering wooden balustraded spire which topped the building until the fire of 1847 was not restored but ten years later in 1857 public subscription raised funds for the installation of the clock. It was installed by Glasgow clockmaker Mr. MacKenzie and was the first turret clock constructed in Scotland on the same principles as the famous Westminster Palace clock at the House of Commons popularly known as Big Ben, with works mainly of cast iron and a new fangled gravity escapement.

The original Burgh Gaol also formed part of the old Town House. A description of it recorded in the Second Statistical Account, published in 1843, reads, 'The state of the prison here has been materially improved within these last few years, under the inspection of the Prison Board. The number of prisoners, confined during last year was 125. This, however, includes the county, and affords no criterion by which to judge the amount of crime in the parish. The prison is well secured, and every attention paid to the health and even the comforts of the prisoners. Each cell is heated with a stove and lighted with gas, regularly cleaned and as well ventilated as the situation of the prison will admit. Each prisoner when brought in is washed and clothed in a prison dress. The diet is excellent, consisting of six ounce bread and a proportion of vegetables, each alternate day, pease or a pint of butter milk. Dinner, ox-head broth, four ounce barley, four ounce bread and a proportion of vegetables, each alternate day, pease brose, fish and potatoes. Supper is the same as breakfast. Provision is also made for the religious instruction of the prisoners. In addition to the services of a chaplain, each cell is also provided with a Testament. Mr. Alison, the governor, instructs the male prisoners and his wife the female prisoners. Many of them appear to value the instruction which they receive and some of them make considerable progress. A new jail is to be immediately erected, in which greater facilities will exist for the exercise of the improved prison discipline.'

The last execution in the county took place at Linlithgow prison in 1857. This was the result of a Saturday night fracas at Boghead Bridge on the road between Bathgate and Armadale in which one of the Maxwell brothers from the miners rows at Durhamtown, now Whitside on the road from Bathgate to Whitburn, was killed. When Armadale's only policeman, P.C. Thomas White arrived on the scene he, single handed and armed only with his baton, arrested three other Durhamtown residents, John McLean, his wife and lodger and charged them with the murder. Handcuffed he marched them back to Armadale's only cell. At first light on the Sunday morning P.C. White summoned help from the police at Bathgate and later that day the three prisoners were transferred to the jail at Linlithgow. It was to be John McLean's last journey, because although the knife with which Maxwell had been stabbed was found on Mrs. McLean, both she and the lodger were subsequently released for want of evidence, while McLean himself was found guilty and hanged.

Harsh conditions also prevailed at Linlithgow's Poor House, which continued to operate until after the Second World War when it was converted into St. Michael's Hospital. Today the modern geriatric unit and adjoining day care centre have a fine reputation, but it took the Linlithgow hospital many years to live down its origins, which is hardly surprising considering the treatment meted out to its first inmates when it opened in 1845. Immediately they entered its doors they were stripped and forced to bath in a huge zinc tub while their clothes were put into a smoke chamber to be deloused. They were then allocated a place in one of the huge dormitories which in total could accommodate almost 300 men. Any improvement in these basic conditions had to be earned. Some men did this by continuing their trade such as shoe making, others gathered fire wood and sold it round the local doors. Earnings could buy the privilege of a small single room, but as they grew older most were forced to return to the grim, gloomy dormitories to die.

While life in nineteenth century Linlithgow was far from easy for the town's poorer inhabitants, the town's more well to do families were prospering, as the substantial villas built at this time such as 'Clarendon', 'Bonnytoun House' and 'Nether Parkley' show and many felt that a growing town such as theirs should have a full scale town hall. The occasion of Queen Victoria's golden jubilee in 1887 was chosen for the laying of the foundation stone on a prominent site on the north side of the High Street to the east of the Cross. The site for the Victoria Hall as it was subsequently appropriately known was gifted to the town by Miss Jessie B. Baird in memory of her brother Dr. George Dallas Baird who practised in Linlithgow for half a century.

The Victoria Hall was designed by Edinburgh architect Mr. Russell Walker in Scottish baronial style complete with soaring towers and turrets, which sadly were removed after the Second World War thus robbing its fine facade of much of its original appearance. The hall, which could seat 800 people including accommodation in the balcony, was completed in 1889 at a cost of £3,800 plus a further £1,500 for the accompanying buildings on either side built in the same impressive style and all paid for by public subscriptions raised in the town. It was officially opened on 23rd December by the famous Liberal politician and future Prime Minister, Lord Rosebery, Lord Lieutenant of Linlithgowshire, who had previously been made a freeman of the town on 24th September 1886.

To begin with the Victoria Hall was well used by the townsfolk with events ranging from dances to flower shows and from band concerts to children's operettas, the latter produced by well known local music teacher Russell Fleming. After the Second World War, going to the pictures was all the rage and the Town Council agreed to Caledonian Associated Cinemas converting the hall into the Ritz Cinema as a previous plan to build a picture house on open land where Stuart House, the Procurator Fiscal's office, was more recently built at the west end of the

The pepper pot witches' hat turrets of the Victorian Hall dominated the High Street, when this view looking east from the Cross was taken almost half a century ago. The lack of traffic is another reminder of this more leisurely age in the town's history.

High Street had been abandoned because of rising costs. To begin with the Council retained the right to take over the hall for concerts, political meetings etc., but in 1956 it finally became a full time cinema with Mr. John Mackay as manager. Films were shown regularly until the 1970s when public taste changed again and it became the local bingo hall. At first, bingo sessions were held midweek with films still on screen at weekends but as television increased its hold and cinema audiences continued to fall it became a full time bingo hall. Finally in the 1980s this fine hall reached the lowest depths of its degradation when public taste having changed yet again it was equipped with automatic gaming machines and re-opened as an amusement arcade despite many local protests. So far all efforts to rescue the hall and restore it as a much needed public facility where the members of LAMP, Linlithgow Amateur Musical Productions, the Linlithgow Players, the local dramatic society and the Linlithgow Arts Guild could present their regular shows in a fit setting, have failed. The fate of the Victoria Hall is a disgrace to Linlithgow

The High Street is seldom as quiet as in this attractive view looking east from the Cross and frequent traffic jams stress the need for additional access to the M9 to avoid heavy vehicles coming through the town.

and it can only be hoped that future generations will save it and restore it to its rightful place in the life of the town.

At the beginning of the nineteenth century there was an ambitious scheme to establish Linlithgowshire's headquarters within Linlithgow Palace. No fewer than three plans were drawn up for the installation of a county hall without interfering in any way with the design and appearance of the Palace and had the backing of such public figures as the Earl of Hopetoun and Sir James Dalyell of the Binns, but the government at Westminster put forward so many difficulties that although the Prince Regent actually agreed to this new lease of life for the Palace, all were finally abandoned on 20th April 1821.

In 1842 Queen Victoria paid her one and only visit to Linlithgow, but failed to visit the Palace and, indeed, failed even to stop to listen to the Provost's carefully prepared speech. It had been arranged that both Provost Dawson of Linlithgow and the Provost of Bathgate should present addresses to the Queen and Prince Albert when they stopped at West Port. An enormous crowd of, it is estimated, over 20,000 people not only from Linlithgow and its surrounding towns and villages but from as far away as Glasgow filled the High Street despite heavy rain. At last the Queen's coach came into sight over the brow of the hill on Falkirk Road but because of the soaking weather the royal couple had the hood of their landau raised to protect them and apparently went straight past the platform party waiting with speeches at the ready at West Port. The royal carriage finally stopped opposite historic West Port House, and Provost Dawson clambered down from the official platform and, speech in hand, tried valiantly to make his way along the High Street but was prevented by the crowd who pushed forward to get a better view of the young Queen and her Prince Consort. While he was still many yards away struggling to get through, the Queen's coach moved off again and continued along the High Street with the determined Provost still in hot pursuit. Fresh horses were waiting at the Cross and the royal party stopped long enough for them to be changed ready for the last lap of their wet journey to Holyrood, but not long enough for poor Provost Dawson, weighed down with his official robes and mantle, to complete his High Street dash. In the end he had to be satisfied with forwarding his address to Edinburgh from where the queen graciously acknowledged it. It is interesting to wonder whether if the weather had been better Victoria might not only have heard Provost Dawson deliver his speech in person, but might also have spared a few more moments to go up the Kirk Gate to see the Palace of her ancestors, or whether the former seat of the Stewarts was deliberately omitted from her itinerary as still possibly too sensitive as at the time less than a hundred years had elapsed since the last Jacobite uprising.

Twenty years later in 1862 another attempt was made to restore the Palace, this time as a Sheriff Court House, but the letter columns of the 'Scotsman' and other newspapers were bombarded with criticisms of the scheme from those who claimed to be interested in Scottish history and it was again abandoned. Instead the Sheriff Court House was erected on the site on the south side of the High Street of the house from which the shot which killed the Regent Moray was fired and where today a fine effigy of the Regent and a plaque mark the spot.

Another plaque in the High Street depicts local pharmacist David Waldie whose discovery of the anaesthetic powers of chloroform in his little wood panelled chemist's shop where the Four Marys Restaurant is now situated, gives Linlithgow another claim to fame. After months of careful experiment, Waldie felt confident enough to send a small sample of chloroform to West Lothian's other medical pioneer, Bathgate born Sir

James Young Simpson, who had by this time established a prosperous practice in Edinburgh's fashionable Queen Street. Simpson tried out the gas on himself and slid unconscious to the floor. When he came to, Simpson realised that he was not suffering from the after effects experienced when using ether, which had been the only anaesthetic available up until that time and soon went on to introduce Waldie's chloroform to ensure safer operations, and less painful child birth. The success of Waldie's discovery was guaranteed when Simpson managed to persuade no less a person than Queen Victoria to allow the use of chloroform at the next royal birth.

As well as progress in medicine, Victorian times also saw advances in education especially after the Education Act of 1872 made schooling compulsory for the first time. In Linlithgow this resulted in the Grammar School being converted into the Burgh Board School but the growing need for secondary education led in 1894 to the opening of the Academy in what is now Longcroft Hall at West Port. The name Linlithgow Academy can still be picked out on the arched recess of the front wall. As a secondary school the Academy was at first fee paying and its staff consisted of only the Rector and his assistant who was referred to as the doctor. Like the Burgh Board School or Grammar School which continued in the Kirk Gate, its curriculum was strictly academic and classical and it offered no practical subjects of any kind.

For most Linlithgow bairns education still came to an end on their thirteenth birthday when they went to work straight from primary school. The largest primary school in the town was situated opposite the Academy in the playground of what is still the West Port Annexe of Linlithgow Primary. It had been founded in 1844 as a church school by the members of the congregation of the Free Church.

As non conformists the congregation of the Free Church evidently felt that they wished their children educated in their own beliefs and started their own school. At first the children attended classes in the pews of the church and were called to their lessons on weekdays by the same bell which summoned the congregation to worship on the Sabbath. The big bell can still be seen as it has been erected at the main entrance to Linlithgow Primary School as a memorial to one of the school's best known headmasters Councillor William Alexander who rescued it when the original buildings at West Port were demolished.

Victorian times were also a time of expansion for the church in Linlithgow and St. Ninians was built and opened in 1874. Situated adjacent to the original Linlithgow Academy in Falkirk Road at West

Port, the old school now serves as church hall. St. Ninians, named after the early Christian missionary who had chapels at Torphichen and Blackness and who brought the faith to the area, is particularly well known for its fine spire which dominates the West Port district of the town. It later merged with Craigmailen Church, which took its name from the farm in the Bathgate Hills in whose fields its Succeeder congregation originally worshipped before erecting their first premises in Linlithgow. Today the Rev. Sam Harris preaches to the joint St. Ninians Craigmailen congregation.

Further up the hill above the town St. John's Evangelical Church's fine well proportioned stone building was erected in 1840, while the town's Scottish Episcopalian congregation opened their church on the south side of the High Street in 1919. Built to a very unusual design with a Byzantine dome, it was originally called St. Mildreds, but it has more recently been rededicated to St. Peter with the Rev. Colin Reid as priest in charge. In 1893 the town's Roman Catholics opened their church at Low Port where Father Ferrari is now priest. They called it St. Michael's in remembrance of the times when their style of worship had held sway at the church which overlooks it from its site on the hill. A Catholic primary school had been opened on an adjacent site to St. Michael's R.C. Church four years earlier on 1st July 1889 and served the Catholic community for over half a century until the new St. Joseph's R.C. Primary was opened in 1964 as part of the Preston Road education campus, where it now celebrates its centenary in 1989 with a visit from the Archbishop.

Up at the original St. Michael's, the nineteenth century also ended with alterations and improvements. Inspired by the dramatic restorations of St. Giles Cathedral in Edinburgh and Dunblane Cathedral, many members of the congregation of St. Michael's felt it was very wrong that their fine old church was robbed of its original Gothic glory, by the partition erected in 1812, which divided it in two and totally destroyed the original medieval concept of the church in the shape of the crucifix made up of nave, chancel, transepts, choir and apse. At the beginning of 1890 these enthusiasts called a meeting of the congregation and a committee was formed to seek ways of financing the restoration. Such was the enthusiasm in the town that donations of over £1,100 were soon received and these were supplemented by a grant of £2000 from the Baird Trust. A bazaar raised a further £1,700, an enormous amount from any sale of work in Victorian times.

By 1894 almost £8000 had been collected and restoration was started with the removal of the galleries. The work took almost two years to complete and St. Michael's was re-opened on 24th October 1896. Minister of the church at the time was the Rev. Dr. John Ferguson. He was very proud of St. Michael's and wrote its history but, sadly, his ministry was also a time of much personal grief. For during his time at St. Michael's Dr. Ferguson lost his two daughters in tragic accidents. One was killed when she fell through the ice on the loch while out skating with her fiancé. The other, nine year old little Esther died on 2nd December 1888 when her long hair caught fire while she dried it in front of the manse fire. The smallest stained glass window in St. Michael's was dedicated to her memory by Dr. and Mrs. Ferguson. It is a beautiful depiction of the boy Samuel kneeling in prayer in the temple and is so situated in the Celtic Chapel on the north side of St. Michael's that when Dr. Ferguson raised his eyes from the pulpit it reminded him of his beloved little daughter.

While the smallest window in St. Michael's is very appropriately dedicated to little Esther, the largest which dominates the eastern end of the apse is equally appropriately dedicated to the great achievements of one of Linlithgow's most famous Victorians, Professor Sir Charles Wyville Thomson of Bonsyde House, now the Earl of Moray Hotel, overlooking the east end of the loch. It was the loch where he used to linger on his way home from school to catch tadpoles, sticklebacks and minnows which is said to have been responsible for Professor Thomson's life long fascination with underwater exploration.

As part of a brilliant academic career, Professor Thomson carried out several underwater expeditions off the coast of Scotland which created great public interest. To the Victorians the mysteries of the sea bed were as fascinating as those of outer space to modern generations and the government was encouraged to finance a round the world voyage to reveal more secrets of the deep. Professor Thomson was invited to lead it and in December 1872 set out on what was to become the world famous 'Challenger' Expedition, named after the naval vessel on which he and his team of scientists sailed from Sheerness. Between steaming out of Sheerness and her return to Spithead three and a half years later in May 1876, the 'Challenger' with her fully equipped laboratories sailed over 70,000 nautical miles and took over 350 soundings at places in the Atlantic, Pacific and Antarctic Oceans reaching depths never before contemplated. The scientific information collected resulted in Professor Thomson being knighted by Queen Victoria. Sadly, the four years of non stop research aboard the 'Challenger' had impaired Sir Charles' health and he died only six years later in 1882.

The Boy Samuel window is the smallest of St. Michael's many beautiful stained glass windows. As indicated by the inscription it was installed by former minister at St. Michael's and the church's historian, the Rev. Dr. Ferguson in memory of his little daughter Esther who died when her hair caught alight as she dried it in front of the open fire in the manse at the top of Manse Road. Esther was the second of the Ferguson girls to die in tragic circumstances during their father's ministry at St. Michael's, her older sister drowning when she fell through the ice on the loch while out skating one winter's evening with her fiancé. With its rich colours the Boy Samuel window has been a popular choice for reproduction on Christmas cards, but St. Michael's does also have a lovely Nativity window.

His colleagues and former students at Edinburgh University decided to mark his achievements by installing a very special stained glass window in the apse at St. Michael's depicting the whole of the universe from the heavens, very appropriately right to the bottom of the sea. It was these latter scenes which obviously particularly interested the many students who attended the service of dedication. At first sight the window was as wonderful and impressive as they could possibly have hoped for, but then their eyes alighted on the sea bed. To their horror they looked again. For there in the corner the artist had included a lobster and it was red, a colour which lobsters only turn after they are boiled. Fortunately a follow-up expedition to that on which Professor Thomson had made his name aboard the 'Challenger' finally saved the artist's blushes because it sent home word that in Australian waters it had discovered a lobster which, if not quite red, was certainly a very satisfactory shade of pink.

St. Michael's many other fine windows are also very much worth while looking at in detail. For instance the flamboyant window in St. Katharine's Aisle, in which both the intricate stone work and the glass were renewed in 1845, is said to bear comparison with the finest stained glass windows in the cathedral in Chartres and may indeed have been carved by a mason from France as one of the masons who built St. Michael's was called French. The St. Katharine's aisle window depicts the text from St. Matthew, chapter 11, verse 28, 'Come unto me' and depicts in vivid colour Jesus welcoming the children. It was gifted to the church by the Dawson family whose father, Adam Dawson, was responsible for supervising the restoration of the stone tracery which took place while he was Provost of the town.

Another window in St. Michael's of particular interest to children is that depicting the nativity scene. Moving further west the window at the foot of the tower portraying the transfiguration of Christ, is best seen at sunset when its colours are shown to advantage. Most interesting of all the windows as far as the history of St. Michael's itself is concerned is the Masonic Window for it not only shows the monarchs with connections with the church but also depicts the church itself at different stages in its development. The saints shown are St. Michael, St. Andrew for Scotland and St. Bridget who is included as patron saint of the Hamilton family who had landowning connections in the area. It is interesting to note that St. Bridget is also remembered in the place name East Kilbride near the Duke of Hamilton's original family home at Hamilton in Lanarkshire.

The Masonic Window with its fine portrait in stained glass of Queen Victoria, is now the dominant feature of the Queen's Aisle, but it is to our present Queen that it is dedicated and was specially created to mark Her Majesty's silver anniversary as monarch in 1987. The very beautiful Queen's Aisle is also designed to provide St. Michael's with a small intimate side chapel suited to private prayer and smaller services. It was

A bride's eye view up the nave of St. Michael's Church to the creation window in the apse. The choir leading to the apse is covered in carpeting specially woven for St. Michael's by Templetons of Glasgow. Rich red in colour and bearing repeated motifs of St. Michael conquering evil in the shape of a dragon, the carpet which is edged by a never ending eternity chain, was guaranteed by the skilled Scottish craftsmen who wove it to improve with age.

designed by the well known local architect, Mr. William Cadell of Grange, who has succeeded admirably in blending this new addition with the ancient church without its introduction being at all intrusive by keeping the new oak screens to a height beneath that of the existing windows and including in them panes of delicately coloured glass which both provide a sense of openness and, when the sun shines, cast a rainbow pattern on the stone flagged floor, reminiscent of the pattern which must once have been cast on the floor of the presence chamber in the nearby Palace. All of the fitments and furnishings in the Queen's Aisle from the tapestry on the communion table to the seats have been lovingly made by members of the congregation and local craftsmen from Linlithgow.

When Her Majesty comes to Linlithgow for the first time since her Coronation tour in the 1950s then it is likely that her attention will be drawn in St. Michael's to the church's magnificent Queen's Pulpit.

Installed in 1896 it is the work of a Glasgow artist, John Honeyman, who supervised the whole of the 1890s restoration and also designed the baptismal font near the south door. The pulpit displays very fine wood carvings of Queen Margaret, wife of King Malcolm Canmore (later St. Margaret), of Mary Queen of Scots and of Queen Victoria. One niche still remains to be filled, however, so perhaps a royal visit would give St. Michael's the ideal opportunity to commission a new statuette of the Queen.

Behind the Queens' Pulpit stands the fine pipe organ added to the church at the time of the 1890s restoration and opposite in the chancel is the magnificent golden eagle lectern gifted to the church at the same time by Lord Linlithgow, Miss Baird (whose generosity has already been mentioned), a Mr. William Gilkison and the minister, Dr. Ferguson. It is said that the lectern was made in the shape of the eagle as it alone of all the birds was strong enough to carry both the Old and New Testaments of the Bible.

Another item of great beauty in St. Michael's is the carpet, specially woven in one piece by Templetons of Glasgow, which stretches from the choir into the apse and which provides a perfect final touch for the many wedding groups for whom the church provides such a breathtaking setting. The scarlet carpet bears the motif of St. Michael overcoming evil by slaying a symbolic dragon and is edged with a never ending Celtic eternity chain in gold.

It leads right up the steps into the apse which is surrounded by excellent examples of modern Scottish craftsmanship in the shape of the stalls made in 1956. The arms are all individually carved and depict many of the animals and birds mentioned in the Bible from the wee kirk mouse to a puddock and from a raven to a little playful monkey. Overhead on the intricately carved canopy appear the lamb of God, and a white dove.

Down the steps to the right the ancient lead cockerel which once looked down over Linlithgow from its perch as St. Michael's weather vane has found a place to roost in the corner beside the war memorial. St. Michael's is unique amongst Scottish churches, not in housing a war memorial, but in the fact that it is the town's memorial to those who fell in the First and Second World Wars whose names are recorded in the Book of Remembrance. Above hang the flags, now practically turned to cobwebs, of the West Lothian regiments and on each Remembrance Sunday the flags of local uniformed organisations are still trooped through the church while, from the open door of the belfry, high above the bugler sounds the last post.

As one of the most impressive places of worship in the whole country it is not surprising that St. Michael's has featured so often on radio and television on programmes ranging from B.B.C. television's well known 'Songs of Praise' to a Christmas Eve Midnight Service conducted by its present minister the Rev. Ian Patterson who, by coincidence, came like his predecessor, Dr. Steel, from St. Andrews, Nairobi to Linlithgow. St. Michael's has also been the setting for productions of Benjamin Britten's 'Noyes Fludde' and of T. S. Eliot's famous drama 'Murder In the Cathedral'.

During the latter production the appearance of the priests in their flowing habits made it comparatively easy to imagine what St. Michael's must have looked like in pre Reformation times and walking away from the war memorial through the Queen's Aisle, it is still possible to see one of the piscinas where the original monks used to wash out the gold communion vessels. Beside it on the wall is an old burial stone which often puzzles visitors as the inscription is written in circles starting at the outer edge and working its way into the centre.

Another interesting circle is the carved stone ring which adorns the middle of the inside of the roof of the vestibule of the south porch and which is a reminder that, before the Reformation this was often the setting for weddings, rather than the church itself. Above the porch is a priest's room with a small oriel window. This little room is reached by a spiral turnpike or newel stair so tight that it is not open for viewing, but the rest of St. Michael's is open most days from 10 a.m. to noon and from 2 p.m. to 4 p.m. And with so much to see it is very much worth visiting.

CHAPTER NINE

The Turn of the Century

THE twentieth century began excitingly for Linlithgow. There was in particular great activity at the Low Port end of the town where work began on the construction of a new factory and on 2nd September 1900, the Earl of Hopetoun came to lay the foundation stone of the new Linlithgow Academy. Both turned out to be surprisingly impressive buildings compared with the hideous monstrosities produced by modern architects and of which the present Linlithgow Academy is a classic example.

The new Nobel Works were completed first in 1901 and with their red brick multi-arched Italian piazza style frontage soon became a well known landmark at the east end of the High Street. Whether or not this interesting industrial design was inspired by Linlithgow's other famous arched piazza which had formerly graced the front of the Town House at the Cross is not known but it is certainly sad that in the 1980s the modern planners allowed such a pleasant feature to be demolished and replaced by one of the most unsightly supermarkets ever built. How such an ugly building was permitted to be erected on such a prime site within a conservation area is as much a mystery as to why the charming old piazza was originally built.

The Nobel Works were part of the industry started by the famous Swedish chemist and engineer, Alfred Nobel, who had died five years earlier in 1896. Considering that he is now best remembered for the Nobel Peace Prizes (which, incidentally, were awarded for the first time in 1901 the year the Linlithgow factory opened) it is somewhat ironic that his company specialised in the manufacture of explosives. Apart from patenting processes for the manufacture of dynamite and for combining nitroglycerin with guncotton to make blasting gelatin, Nobel was also responsible for finding out how to make safety fuses so that his explosives could be detonated safely and it was these which were at first manufactured in Linlithgow. On the outbreak of the First World War, however, production at the Low Port factory was quickly switched to making ammunitions for use at the front despite the risks of explosions which this must have involved. The Nobel Works or the 'Explosives Factory' as they became known became one of the largest employers of female workers in the area and women used to travel in from surrounding towns and villages such as Bridgend and Avonbridge. During World War Two an explosion killed five of the six women working in the incendiary department. The one survivor although badly injured recovered and lives in Avonbridge.

Later the Nobel Works switched to the production of pharmaceutical goods and were purchased by Britain's largest company Imperial Chemical Industries. During this time the factory was known by its correct name of the Regent Works, in memory of the Regent Moray who had been assassinated in the High Street and the eventual closure by I.C.I. as part of the chemical giant's rationalisation plan during the 1960s was a severe blow to Linlithgow's economy. Many local workers subsequently moved south to I.C.I.'s other factories in Macclesfield and other parts of Cheshire.

When the Regent works were finally demolished to make way for the present Regent Shopping Centre, which retains the name, a time capsule, buried as part of the opening ceremony in 1901, was unearthed. After its contents had been examined they were replaced and a second capsule filled with similar items such as local and national newspapers and coins of the 1980s was buried alongside it in the middle of the shopping precinct courtyard.

Time capsules must have been very much in fashion at the beginning of this century, because a similar one was also placed in a hollow stone at the laying of the foundation ceremony across the road at the then new Linlithgow Academy. The Academy's handsome Scottish baronial style complete with towers and central roof top cupola was the work of architect Graham Fairley. It took builders Richard and William Philip two years to complete in sandstone with grey slate roof and cost £7000. Defying superstition, 13th June 1902 was chosen as the opening day and Rector James Beveridge led his 52 pupils in procession along the High Street from the school's original premises at Longcroft Hall. They were accompanied by the local pipe band and the High Street was decked

The viaduct carrying the railway line across the valley of the Avon is depicted on the sign at the Bridge Inn, Linlithgow Bridge's popular hostelry, whose foresteps make a convenient platform for the proposing of toasts on Marches Day each June. The welcome at the old inn is equally warm throughout the rest of the year and it is well known for its excellent home cooking.

with flags for the big occasion. By this time the staff of the Academy had grown from two to six and it had such a good reputation that, despite still being fee paying, pupils used to walk from as far away as Bo'ness to attend its classes. Amongst them was Jimmy Kidd from Carriden House who later went on to become Linlithgowshire's Unionist Member of Parliament. 'The Carriden Kid' as he was popularly nicknamed held the seat until he was eventually defeated in a bitterly fought contest against Labour's famous Emanuel Shinwell.

Mr. Kidd's daughter Margaret later brought further fame to the family when she was appointed Scotland's first woman Sheriff and later became a Dame of the British Empire. She was honoured by Linlithgow in 1968 when invited to return to perform the opening ceremony at Linlithgow Academy's third building at Braehead, urgently needed by then to accommodate the school's roll of 900 which subsequently increased to over 1000. (Dame Margaret died in March 1989).

Back in 1902, the year which saw the Academy move to its second set of buildings at Low Port also, by a strange coincidence, saw the end of Linlithgow's historic Grammar School. The big one-roomed school with its mullioned windows, situated through the arch in the Kirk Gate where the Rose Garden is now sited, still depended on an open fire for its heating. On the evening of 25th February 1902 the big fire may not have been properly put out when classes ended on that dark winter afternoon and early the following morning the old school caught fire. Although the town's volunteer firemen rushed up the hill from their engine house in the bottom floor of the Town House, there was little they could do to save the school as the water supply was frozen. Next morning Rector Forbes, or 'Auld Rusty Beard' as he was more often called by his pupils, found himself without a school. The children's delight at the abandonment of classes was short lived because they were soon merged with the pupils at the Academy and the ruins of the Grammar School were demolished.

From the fact that, even including the boys from the Grammar School, the total roll of the Academy when it moved later that year to Low Port was still only 52, it is clear that as yet very few Linlithgow youngsters enjoyed the privilege of a secondary education. Even when the school leaving age was raised they did not all go to the Academy until 1929 as before then all but the most able were catered for in the supplementary classes of Linlithgow Public School, the predecessor of the present Linlithgow Primary.

Linlithgow Public occupied the site opposite West Port between Falkirk and Lanark Roads originally used by the pupils of the Free Church School started in 1844. At the beginning of this century its roll was expanding rapidly and although its infant pupils still occupied the partitioned church hall (as they continued to do until the opening of the new Linlithgow Primary at Preston Road in 1967) new premises were urgently needed for the older scholars. These were opened in 1903 and, with their central assembly hall with its magnificent wooden beamed roof like the hull of an upturned sailing ship, still to this day serve Linlithgow Primary's oldest pupils. Up until 1929 only the ablest lads and lassies o' pairts went on to the Academy. Time tables for the supplementary classes for the boys and girls over the age of twelve who remained at the Public at West Port still survive and show time allocated for moral education, two minutes each session for physical education to be performed in the classroom corridors between the desks and periods devoted not to the teaching of geography but to studying the Empire! In connection with this links were soon forged with the colonies through the school in Lithgow, New South Wales and an Australian flag, sent by the latter, was proudly hoisted on the flag pole at West Port. The two schools have recently resumed their correspondence and an Australian flag is again flown at West Port.

Another link with Australia, of which Linlithgow was particularly proud at this time, was the Lord Lieutenant of the County, John Hope, seventh Earl of Hopetoun who was also that country's first Governor-General and a statue of him in all his viceroy's finery was erected at the Cross. Made of bronze it weathered badly and attempts to clean it only made things worse so that in 1970 the 'Green Man' as it had become known popularly in the town was relegated to a new site tucked away in the Rose Garden where it can still be seen.

Another member of the Hope family also remembered in Linlithgow is General Sir John Hope, afterwards Earl of Hopetoun, who was second in command to the famous General Moore in the Peninsula Campaign during the Napoleonic War. General Hope took command of the British forces when Moore was killed at the Battle of Corunna and subsequently successfully supervised what has become known as the Dunkirk of the Napoleonic period. On his return home, very much the hero of his time, Hope's portrait was painted by the celebrated Henry Raeburn and is on display in Old County Buildings.

Although officially deemed 'Old', the County Buildings occupying the long narrow site at right angles to the High Street just to the west of the Cross is, by Linlithgow standards comparatively new, dating only from 1940, when it replaced the original County Hall now one of the Burgh Halls in the Kirk Gate. The term 'Old' has been added to its title simply to indicate that it has been replaced as West Lothian's seat of government by the District Council's new headquarters over the hills in Bathgate. Old County Buildings is, however, still an impressive building well worth a quick visit to see not only the Victorian paintings of the Hopes of Hopetoun House and of Lord Rosebery of Dalmeny House but also the new portrait in oils of Tam Dalyell of the Binns. Painted by Victoria Crowe in 1987, it was specially commissioned to mark the twenty-fifth anniversary of Mr. Dalyell's election as a Member of Parliament and his years of service to the district which are very much recognised by most of his constituents, no matter what their political views. At first Tam Dalyell represented West Lothian, but now Linlithgow is a Parliamentary constituency in its own right adding to the town's distinction of being both the site of the District and Sheriff Courts, the later of which occupies fine Victorian premises next to Old County Buildings. To make way for the erection of the County Buildings at the beginning of World War Two, an old High Street tenement had to be demolished and this exposed the western gable of the British Linen Bank Building which was subsequently dressed with stone from Craigleith Quarry. One stone was carved with the bank's initials, BLB, and it can still be seen high on the side wall, although the bank which it represents disappeared many years ago from the Scottish business scene. The premises then became the well known headquarters of West Lothian Education Authority with chairmen such as Councillors Gavin Howieson, John Graham and Jimmy Boyle, deciding the promotion prospects of many an aspiring dominie while exercising an almost patriarchal interest over both teachers and pupils alike. Much joked about at the time, with the coming of Regionalisation, such an interest is sadly missed.

While the British Linen Bank, which started in the premises overlooking the Cross, is now but a merged memory, a few yards further east along the High Street the most impressive bank buildings ever erected in Linlithgow are still used for trading but now under the banner of the Royal Bank of Scotland. Built in 1859 as the Commercial Bank, the Royal Bank's premises were deliberately built like a castle, complete with stone tower fortified with imitation cannon, as a visible sign to local investors of the bank's security and solidarity. At a time when many people believed that the money which they deposited was actually kept on the premises a further guarantee of the safety of their investments was that the manager or Bank Agent as he was called in Victorian times lived with his family directly above the safe in one of the finest houses in the High Street on the first and second floors of the building.

Another substantial and attractive building, again with decorative turret, added to the High Street scene was the Post Office which moved into its fine new stone premises in 1904, having previously been situated at the Cross. To make way for the new Post Office, complete with its spacious sorting office, situated so conveniently close to the railway station, the old Greenyards cottages and tenement were demolished thus removing yet another link with Linlithgow's past. But at the time this was considered to matter little as Linlithgow moved confidently and prosperously forward into the new century.

Another sign that Linlithgow was indeed moving with the times was that although the new Post Office had been sited with rail transport in mind, garages were opening up to cater for the new fangled petrol driven motor cars. One was set up at Low Port on Blackness Road while, right

Hamilton's Land at the east end of the High Street is now happily preserved for posterity by the National Trust for Scotland as part of its Little Houses Scheme. The houses are private homes and are not open to the public. This picture shows Hamilton's Land at 38 High Street in the days when the popular Victory Cafe occupied the ground floor.

The Red Lion Inn began life as the Golden Lion. Why it changed colour is a mystery, but what is certain is that it has always been one of the town's most popular hostelries from the days when it was a coaching inn to the present day. One of its attractions used to be a skittle alley. Next door can be seen historic Hamilton's Land, now the Linlithgow Bookshop, one of the National Trust for Scotland's little houses in the High Street, with its red pantiled roof, its little doocot in the eaves and its crow step gable which in typically Dutch fashion was built end on to the street.

next door to the Post Office on the south side of the High Street, Donaldson's Garage installed what is claimed to have been the very first petrol pump in Scotland in 1919.

Before then the drivers of Linlithgow's few privately owned motor cars had to go to local ironmongers such as Gillespies to buy petrol. The first shop in the whole district to stock fuel being the little general store in the village of Newton on the road between Linlithgow and South Queensferry. The petrol was brought by horse drawn cart from Leith Docks to the old whitewashed shop, which can still be seen beside the Newton Filling Station, especially to supply the area's first motor car owner, the Earl of Linlithgow who sent his chauffeur from Hopetoun House to collect the cans.

For most people in the district, however, their first experience of petrol driven transport came from travelling on Linlithgow's first buses. Two in number they were, at first, locally owned by the Henderson family but were taken over in 1923 by the Scottish Motor Traction Company — the famous S.M.T. — which opened a depot opposite the Cross and which, under a variety of names and guises, has provided services throughout the whole area ever since. The familiar letters S.M.T. survived right through the Second World War, even when its vehicles' familiar green was replaced by utility grey, and on into the 1950s when the name was first changed to Scottish Omnibuses. Later, it became Eastern Scottish but the biggest change of all did not occur until 1987 when, to fight deregulation of bus transport, which allowed other local private bus operators to challenge it for routes, reorganisation brought the Linlithgow bus depot under the control of Midland Scottish, the successors of Falkirk's famous Alexanders Coach Company. Alexanders were, of course, particularly well known for their 'Bluebirds' and in keeping with this livery the change to Midland Scottish has brought until now unfamiliar blue buses to Linlithgow's routes. Another change brought about by the deregulation of public bus services has been the introduction for the first time of mini buses on several routes including those to Springfield and Riccarton.

The coming of regular bus services in the early 1920s made Linlithgow a popular shopping centre for the surrounding country villages and the posher residents of Bo'ness even travelled over the Flints to shop as the county town was considered to have a better class of grocers. These included Jamieson, Grocer and Wine Merchant; Hutton, Provision and Spirit Merchant; McNairs, Drinnans, and Philips, who were all also licensed to sell beers, wines and spirits. McNairs offered its own blend of whisky produced at St. Magdalene's Distillery, while Drinnans promised whisky by the gallon! Beer was also brewed locally at the old Maltings in Mains Road, whose distinctive turreted building has been saved from demolition and turned into flats.

For those who perhaps imbibed too freely Linlithgow had two chemists. They were Thomas Lumsden, at 17 High Street and C. M. Spence, at 133 and 135 High Street. Both shops were lined with highly polished dark wooden shelves on which were displayed the drugs in their blue bottles and phials from which the chemist dispensed the pills and powders needed to fulfill each individual prescription issued by the local G.P.s. To keep his customers healthy Lumsden, who had previously worked for the famous Edinburgh chemists, Duncan Flockart and Company, also advertised that he could supply 'Linlithgow's aerated waters, special quality mineral waters made from the famous and ancient well of the Crusaders, the Knights Templar.' Mention of the Knights of St. John is a reminder that they owned several tenements in the High Street which were still known as the Templar Lands until they were taken over by the town council. Apart from Lumsden Linlithgow's other chemists, C. M. Spence also had a branch shop at 67 High Street near the Cross where, as well as medicines, they had departments selling stationery and newspapers together with 'a large selection of photographic views of the district, *The History of Linlithgow, Guide to the Palace*' 'Walks round the Roman Wall' and other local publications in addition to daily and weekly newspapers and periodicals. Subscribers' papers punctually delivered', their advertisement promised.

Shops in the High Street also included several drapers with Alexander McDonald at 213, 'Clothier Milliner, Dress and Mantle Maker' and Ballantine's at 121, who claimed that they 'always carried on hand a very large stock of ladies' jackets, mantles and millinery of the finest choice and at the lowest cash prices.' Stobie's shoe shop opened for business for the first time on Christmas Day 1928 and Ian Stobie continues to trade from the same premises today.

The Linlithgow ladies may well have worn their latest dresses and their hand made new hats when they went out for afternoon tea. In the High Street, two establishments offered this daily delight. One tearoom belonged to Haig and Blake, Bakers and Confectioners, who produced 'home baking for visitors and excursionists calling at the tea room opposite the Cross Well.' The other tea room was the Miss Drawbells' Victoria Restaurant, adjacent to the Victoria Hall.

For those who wanted stronger refreshments the High Street was liberally supplied with public houses. In addition to those already mentioned there were, by the 1920s, The Auld Hole In The Wa', Ye Olde Cunzie Neuk, which was also known as the Cross Tavern, the Masonic Arms and the Volunteer Arms. Pubs were, of course, practically exclusively the preserve of the menfolk. Also catering for the gentlemen of Linlithgow was the Victoria Hairdressing Saloon, adjoining the Victoria Hall where according to its advertisements, 'every attention is paid to the comfort and convenience of customers, who may also purchase cigars of choice brand, cigarettes and tobacco, as well as a large assortment of pipes.'

Pipes of a larger variety were the speciality of P. G. Fleming, Plumber and Gas Fitter, who could supply, 'sanitary appliances on the newest and most approved principals as well as gas stoves and incandescent lights.' The gas for the stoves and lights was produced at the Linlithgow Gas Works situated on the shores of the Loch at the Old Water Yett near the

Vennel. Fleming's rival in town were the Bo'ness based Dymock Brothers who as well as undertaking all kinds of plumbing jobs also sold from their Linlithgow branch, 'Non Pareil wringers and mangles all fitted with rubber rollers, guaranteed to be of solid white rubber throughout.' The rubber was also guaranteed not to 'slip on the spindle' and 'a rubber roller recovery service' was also provided.

The largest industry in the Linlithgow area John G. Stein and Co. Ltd. of Manuel, was founded during this period in 1928 bringing many men and their families to the town in the depressed twenties and produced its first bricks in 1930. Since then Stein's has grown to be the world's top producer of refractory materials and recently received the Queen's Award for exports, which are shipped regularly to over one hundred and forty countries. The export demand for the company's products is an indication of the high quality of the company's Super Duty Fire Bricks, which contain over 43 per cent alumina, some of it mined on site. In addition the factory makes special refractories based on imported high alumina, chrome and magnesite ores. All of the bricks are fired in enormous seven hundred foot long gas or oil fired tunnel kilns which are the largest of their kind in the world. Today Stein's employs six hundred and ten workers, many of them from Linlithgow.

Linlithgow at this period was very much a sporting town. In winter curling was the sport. Whenever the ice on the loch was thick enough to be bearing, bonspiels were quickly organised. They proved colourful affairs with thick rugs and well filled hip flasks as necessary equipment as the heavy granite stones rumbling over the ice gave curling its nickname of 'The Roaring Game'. Matches were also organised on the stretch of the Union Canal opposite Rosemount Park but these were liable to be rudely interrupted by the arrival of the ice breaking barge pulled by anything up to ten or a dozen big Clydesdale horses with lots of the town's bairns cheering on their efforts. Rather than take this risk or, indeed, wait for the ice to be thick enough, most games were therefore played on the artificial curling rink situated behind the Burgh Halls, which existed until recent years, and where water was sprayed onto the tarmacadamed surface where during the winter months it froze to form a suitably slippery surface. Another man-made curling pond still exists in the grounds of the Grange but, unlike the one behind the Burgh Halls, it always depended on the freezing over of its shallow waters, before the Cadell family could invite their guests to form rinks and take to the ice.

In summer curling was replaced by quoiting, a sport in which the aim was to throw horse shoes over targets set in sand. There were several

Linlithgow has always had a good record in athletics as this picture of the local harriers taken in 1921 shows. The runner crouching on the left is Alex Dumbreck. A member of the well known Linlithgow family, whose brother Jimmy has returned to live in the High Street after serving with distinction in India and gaining the O.B.E. for his services in establishing Ghana as an independent country, he was always known locally as Echie.

quoiting rinks behind pubs in the High Street and like curling it had the reputation of being a somewhat drouthy sport.

Golf was played on the West Lothian Course on the crest of Erngath Hill with the Hope Monument, erected to the memory of Adrian Hope of Hopetoun House who died during the siege of Fort Rooah during the Indian Mutiny, a well known monument in its centre. The West Lothian Course, built on lands belonging to the neighbouring House of Grange, existed long before Mrs. Gina MacKinnon of Williamscraig and Drambuie fame very generously gave land beside the Union Canal for Linlithgow's own golf club.

Cricket in Linlithgow was originally played in the picturesque setting of the Peel and local legend still lovingly recalls the day when the mighty Bamberry, the town halberdier and bell-ringer went in to bat and hit one ball so far that it landed against the Palace wall! Other hazards which hindered similar big hitters such as Bailies Jimmy Borthwick and David

Morrison, included a huge tree near the wicket which, as it grew in the Royal Park, could not be removed, and the loch, where a rowing boat had to be kept at the ready to rescue balls which landed in the water.

Thus, when in 1928 cricket clubs throughout the county came together to found the West Lothian County Cricket Association, even the staunchest Black Bitches amongst its members had to agree reluctantly that despite its perfect setting with its natural amphitheatre, the Peel could not meet the standards required for cricket at this level. At first the new club considered creating a pitch at Bathgate, but fortunately for Linlithgow, the proposed site was threatened by mining subsidence and so local farmer, Mr. A. F. Gardiner of Springfield, was asked for the lease of his field at Boghall.

Boghall was ready for play by the late spring of 1930 and the first home championship match was played there against Stirlingshire on 31st May and Linlithgow's cricketing authority, James B. Wilson records in his book, 'Fifty Years of Cricket', published in 1979, how West Lothian won by 62 runs to 44, the club's professional Charlie Benham, formerly of Essex, taking six for fifteen and Aleck Ford, three for twenty-seven. Other famous names over the past sixty years at Boghall have included, amongst others, two other Fords, Aleck's sons, Malcolm and Donald, also of football fame, and Charlie Benham's sons, Fred, Maurice and Arthur, as well as Andrew and John Raeburn, Jimmy Fleming, Jimmy Newton, John Gordon, Andrew Johnston, Neil and Jim Wilkie, Jimmy Kidd, Tommy Ingram, Tom Steele, Willie Mackay, Frank Baillie, George Strachan, Lord Dalmeny, John Brock, Willie Ellis, Bert Philip, Tommy Watson, Jim Shanks, Jimmy Lidster, John Clark, George Bannerman, Peter Reid, John Mathieson, John Burns, John Shanks, David Morrison Jnr., Duncan McLaren, Angus Sharp, Sandy Paris (who is a past president and is now honorary president) and current president Sandy Smart of Loch House Farm. Others who will always be remembered as supporters include Cecil Kerr, Jimmy Dumbreck, Tom Kerr, Leslie Gordon, Sandy Nicol, Bill Smith, Sandy Bennie, Jock Smith and David Lunn, as well as many loyal lady members who have provided great support behind the scenes.

All this commitment at Boghall brought particular success during the 1960s, when West Lothian were runners-up in the Counties Championship in 1963 and 1964 and finally won it for the first time in 1965, making it a great year of victories for Linlithgow, as the Rose also won the Scottish Junior Cup! The Boghall players who won the championship were team captain J. M. C. Ford, D. C. C. Ford, D. B. Cairns, J. B. Thomson, D. J. Oliphant, G. M. Bannerman, P. L. Fraser, T. Williamson, V. Harris, G. R. Strachan, K. M. Lawson, A. Raeburn, J. B. Wilson, J. Lidster and P. M. Reid, and Provost Baird honoured them with a civic reception.

The Scottish Counties Championship was won again in 1984, with George Bannerman who had played in 1965, again in the winning team which was captained by Bruce Dixon who is once more captain for the 1989 season. Linlithgow's cricketing enthusiasts have always done much to encourage youngsters in the town to take up the game and, as well as junior elevens which practise faithfully weekly throughout the season, the Association also organises the new 'team cricket' (8-a-side Softball) for pupils at the primary schools in and around the town, Lowport Primary's team going forward to the SCU National Tournament as holders of the F. C. Benham Memorial Trophy at Perth in 1987 and 1988. With all this interest and a pool of fine young players at Boghall, including Scottish internationalists Ken Scott and David Fleming, the future of cricket in Linlithgow seems well assured.

Boghall's green turf was also the scene of annual school summer sports and athletics. Racing of a very different type took place later at Mains Park where a popular greyhound racing track was established during the early 1940s and attracted dogs from Bo'ness, Bathgate, Armadale and other neighbouring towns for its weekly meetings at which the bookies did a roaring trade.

More up market racing took place once a year as it still does on a Spring Saturday when the Linlithgow and Stirlingshire Hunt stages its annual point to point meeting at Oatridge. With racing over the jumps, outsiders frequently win, but in years gone by Linlithgow folk often put their money on a favourite from Craigie Brown's stables at the east end of the Loch. During the winter months the Linlithgow and Stirlingshire Hunt also held regular meets in the Bathgate Hills often meeting beforehand to enjoy a stirrup cup in front of the Star and Garter.

During the winter, too, was the time for football and Linlithgow has always been a football stronghold, with Tommy Walker of Hearts fame first being spotted by Mr. Wood, a Linlithgow talent scout who walked all the way to Livingston to see the young man in action. Like Hearts, Linlithgow's favourites wear maroon strips.

Originally, however, the Linlithgow team wore black and white and that original strip was purchased exactly one hundred years ago. For as

The Rose team who won the Scottish Junior Cup in 1965, which proved a year of victories for Linlithgow as the West Lothian County Cricket Association based at Boghall also won the County Championship. This picture shows the Rosie Posies not in their famous maroon strip which they wore proudly at Hampden Park on the winning day, but in a black and white strip which they had to don for the next match after the final when this photograph was taken, to avoid a clash of colours.

the town celebrates the six hundredth anniversary of its becoming a Royal Burgh, Linlithgow Rose and its enthusiastic supporters look forward to celebrating the centenary of their popular club.

The honour of founding Linlithgow's first organised football team goes to the son of Linlithgow's Town Clerk, Mr. Russell, who started the club with a donation of half a crown (12½p). His friends added their contributions and when they had all of twenty four shillings (£1.20) they travelled to Edinburgh and purchased the first black and white strip from Lumley's Sport Shop.

Matches were at first played at Captain's Park, which was situated at the east end of the town, and games were played there regularly throughout the last decade of the nineteenth century. Perseverance and practice finally paid off in 1902 when the team won its first trophy at Tynecastle Park in Edinburgh, by defeating Inverkeithing Thistle in the final of the Forth League Cup. Linlithgow went wild with delight when the team returned with the long awaited trophy and the whole town turned out to welcome the jubilant players, Linlithgow Reed Band turning out, too, to play them along the whole length of the High Street.

Three years later the Linlithgow team won the County Cup with a win in the final over Vale of Grange. In 1914 the much prized Lumley Cup came to Linlithgow but it took six hours of hard fought football to overcome Portobello Thistle.

After the First World War in the 1920s all of the county teams came together to form the West Lothian Junior League and the Rose won the first competition. The 1925-26 season was a particularly good one for the Rose as they won the much coveted Thornton Shield by defeating Musselburgh by one goal to nil in the final at Easter Road and then went on to win the West Lothian County Cup. This latter result was cherished particularly as it involved beating local rivals, Bo'ness Cadora.

The following 1926-27 season proved even more successful for the Rose as they won three trophies, the St. Michael's, the Brown, and the County Cup.

In 1930 the Rose moved their headquarters to the opposite end of the town to the Mains Park on the Bathgate Road. To mark the opening of their new ground they invited Bonnyrigg Rose Athletic and went on to celebrate by beating the visitors by nine goals to one. It was to Mains Park in the following year 1931 that the Rose brought their most famous signing, a slip of a lad from Livingston Village, called Tommy Walker. Club Secretary David Roy still has the club's financial records which show that on 1st June 1931 Tommy Walker's signing fee was £3. 2. 0d. Less than a year later young Walker was signed by the Heart of Midlothian and the transfer fee was all of £35!

Tommy Walker was soon capped for Scotland and many Rose fans still remember the penalty kick he took against England. It was a very windy day and Walker, who was still only in his 'teens, entrusted to take the vital kick, had to replace the ball several times as the wind blew it off the spot. As the tension mounted he finally shot and placed the ball in the net to give Scotland one of its most famous victory's against the auld enemy.

The other old enemy Bo'ness Cadora could always be relied upon to pull in the crowd when they travelled over The Flints to play at Mains Park and the financial records show that their match against the Rose brought in a gate of over £30 compared with £10 against Ormiston and £19 against Dalkeith. Equally interesting are the outgoings recorded in the financial records which range from 1s 0d for a bag of sawdust to mark the pitch to 5s 0d for washing the strips. Buses to take the team to away matches were always hired from W. H. Boyd and costs ranged from £2 to £4 depending on the distance.

At the outbreak of the Second World War, the Rose like many other

F

Junior clubs was forced to close down because of a lack of both players and officials, who were called away to the forces. Mains Park was sold and converted into a greyhound racing stadium, but even before the war was over a few enthusiasts began fund raising to ensure that the club would start again as soon as the boys came home.

In March 1946 a meeting was called to reform the club and it was announced that there was £250 in the funds. The newly elected committee started to work to find suitable new premises. The late ex-Provost A. C. Ford reported that enquiries for a piece of ground which ran alongside the A9 road near Stockbridge had been made but that although the ground was most suitable for a football pitch the Ministry of Transport objected that crowds coming and going to and from matches could cause inconvenience to traffic.

Enquiries shifted to examine a piece of ground between the cemetery and the Gowan Stank Glue Works, but although the area was available the price was too high. Eventually after much haggling a price was agreed and the land was purchased. Much work was required to get the ground into shape but a small army of supporters set to to lay the foundations for what is now regarded as the finest junior pitch in Scotland. Amongst those who laboured hardest to form the new ground were Jock Smith and his son Freddie, Jimmy Cobban, George Trew, Willie McNeish, John Kellock, Joe McCrystal, W. Joyce and Jock Campbell.

At a meeting on 6th March 1947 a vote was taken to choose a name for the new ground. Names proposed were Campbell Park, Preston Park and Gowanstank Field. Gowanstank was chosen but two years later at a committee meeting on 26th May 1949 another vote changed the name to the now much more familiar Prestonfield. Later that same summer on 1st August the Rose played their first competitive match for ten years. It was an away match against Forth Rangers but as the Grangemouth team's ground was not ready for play it took place at First Park, Falkirk, the home of East Stirling.

Less than a week later the big day came for the first match at Prestonfield against Broxburn Athletic. The Rose team lined up with Kinghorn in goal, full backs Jack and Brown, halfbacks Frame, Munro and Flavell, and forwards Boyd, Cameron, Ingles, Bissett and Rankin, Harry Bissett being the only local boy in the side. The match turned out to be a bit of a disappointment for the enthusiastic Rose fans as their favourites lost by five goals to one.

The committee at the time consisted of President A. C. Ford, Secretary John Campbell, Treasurer George Trew, N. Joyce, A. Murdoch, J. Reid,

J. Smith, F. Smith, J. Ross, J. McHugh, J. Ferguson, J. Cobbaw, W. McNeish, J. McCrystal, T. Wallace and J. Ritchie and although the result was a let down they were delighted with the gate of 3000, a ground record which held until 1965 when a crowd of 3536 attended a Fifth Round Scottish Junior Cup match against Shettleston Juniors. A few years later in a Junior Cup tie versus Petershill Juniors a crowd of 3626 attended and this figure holds the crowd record for Prestonfield to the present day.

It took the newly formed Rose until the 1953-54 season to win their first trophies. That season the Rose reached the final of the East of Scotland Cup and travelled to Tynecastle for the big game where they tied one all against Fauldhouse. The replay took place at Volunteer Park, Armadale and this time the Rose made no mistake, winning by four goals to one. A few weeks later at Creamery Park, Bathgate they won the final of the Thornton Shield by defeating Broxburn Athletic.

The next ten years were not so successful for the Rose and by the start of the 1964-65 season the club's funds were down to under £100. Fortunately measures ranging from selling a player, the late Thomas Hamilton to Kilsyth Rangers for £100 to selling scrap steel left over from the building of the enclosure and holding a garden fete at the ground, stabilised the financial situation because at that moment the Rose's fortune suddenly turned.

The season got off to a flying start when the team made up of a mixture of experienced players and young newcomers, beat old rivals Bo'ness United away from home at Newtown Park by three goals to one. This started an amazing run of thirty nine wins in a row without a single defeat. The climax came in 15th May 1965 when at Hampden Park, Glasgow before a 35,000 crowd the Rose, skippered by Tommy Reston, defeated Baillieston Juniors by four goals to one. The team that proud day consisted of McGlynn, Reston, Syme, Veitch, Grant, Gardner, Henderson, Grant, Cowie, Fordyck and Oliphant with the goals being scored by Oliphant, Grant, Gardner and Cowie. That same season apart from one competition, the Rose swept the board adding to the Scottish Junior Cup, the Edinburgh District League Championship, the Brown Cup, the Lanark, Lothian Cup, and the East of Scotland Cup. The only trophy which escaped was the St. Michael's Cup and in that competition the Rose reached the semi-final only to lose to Armadale Thistle by three goals to one and, ironically, it was a Linlithgow lad, Colin Stein, who was mainly responsible for their defeat as he scored all of the goals in the Dale's win.

Linlithgow Rose again reached the final of the Scottish Junior Cup in 1974 but this time despite good playing by local lads, Robert McMeechan, Les Donaldson, and Tommy Ure, who each gave fourteen years service to the club, they lost to Cambuslang.

Rose players who have been capped for Junior Scotland include Charlie Notman, Bobby Veitch, Colin Grant from Bo'ness who scored 54 goals during the Scottish Cup winning year and subsequently went on to play for Hibernian at the end of that season, the other Colin Grant, who was capped in 1981. Colin Sinclair, Ian McLaren, Tommy Ure, who almost became the most capped Junior player in Scotland, John Lapsley, Allan Docherty, Ian Wildridge, Norman Brown, Tommy McGeogh, Hugh McCann, M. Reynolds, G. Clark, and R. Craw. Rose's team coach, John Binnie was appointed manager of Junior Scotland and the team's physiotherapist Bobby Kirk became the Scottish team trainer.

Linlithgow Rose during its one hundred years existence has been equally well served off the field by local men including past President Louis Laurie, present President William Russell (who joined the club in 1958 and has given over thirty years continuous service) Pat Scullion, who has served on the committee for thirty six years and organised many of the club's fund raising schemes, Matt Dick, Director of G. R. Steins Refractories, who is Honorary President and David Roy, the Club Secretary, who supplied all of the information for this section of this book. Mr. Roy joined Linlithgow Rose as secretary in 1959 and has thus completed thirty years of service during which he has been honoured by being appointed President of the Scottish Junior Football Association, a post which he held for five years starting in 1976. He is also a life member of the Scottish Football Association, the Scottish Junior F.A. and the Eastern Region of Scotland Junior F.A.

In 1988 Linlithgow Rose won the Edinburgh and District League Championship and so look well set to continue the proud record which they have established over the past century.

CHAPTER TEN

The War Years

IN 1939 Linlithgow had a population of 3,666 according to the Automobile Association handbook for that year which advised its motoring members that they might stay in the town at the St. Michael's Hotel for five shillings a night, with high tea available daily for only half a crown, or dinner to order for three shillings and six pence.

Like the rest of Scotland, Linlithgow enjoyed a long hot summer, but the beautiful weather failed to inspire the cricketing enthusiasts out at Boghall where, unlike in 1938 when the West Lothian County side came runners up in the County Championship, they had, according to the 'Gazette', a decidedly disappointing season, apart from Sandy Paris' selection to play for Scotland against the M.C.C.

West Lothian's match on Saturday 2nd September against Stenhousemuir ended in yet another draw, but it is still remembered today because although, as they made their way home neither players or supporters realised, it was to be the last competitive game played at Boghall for more than six long years.

For the next morning, as families in Linlithgow, like those in cities, towns and villages throughout the whole of Great Britain, clustered round their wireless sets, Prime Minister Neville Chamberlain declared war against Germany and life was never to be quite the same again.

As far as the children of Linlithgow were concerned the declaration of war simply meant a very welcome extension of the summer holidays, because West Lothian Education Committee hurriedly decided that schools should not re-open as planned on the following Tuesday morning in case the Germans carried out a series of bombing raids. All teachers were, however, ordered to report for duty and the logbook for Linlithgow

Public School describes how they were kept fully occupied preparing ration ·books and preparing lists of homes which might take evacuees form the cities.

By the following week no German planes had been sighted apart from a reconnaissance raid over the Forth Bridge, but the authorities still thought it prudent that the pupils should not return to their classrooms until air raid shelters were built.

While the youngsters continued to enjoy their new found freedom climbing through the wheat fields up the slopes of Cockleroi, picnicking in the Peel, paddling in the loch and, perhaps, in time honoured fashion, testing their manhood by leaping the horse trough beneath Katie Wearie's tree, their teachers worried about the damage being done to their education by this absence from their books. A plan was therefore devised in the staffroom at West Port and selected pupils from different areas of the town were summoned to bring their bikes to school. Using these luckless cyclists a homework on wheels scheme was duly set in motion, lessons being sent out one day and ferried back the next.

Two months later with still no sign of the expected blitz it was decided that all pupils must return to school on 6th November on a reduced day basis from 9.30 to 3 p.m. and this continued until the air raid shelters were finished. The completion of the shelters in the West Port playground brought the first test of the gas masks, which had been issued as a precaution to the boys and girls in 1938, and soon proved that many had outgrown them and the teachers had to organise a new distribution. While the children at Linlithgow Public tried out their new brick built and concrete roofed shelters, their big brothers and sisters at the other end of the town in the Academy at Lowport were marched over the little bridge across the burn and through the Peel, because it had been decided that the safest place for them was deep in the cellars of the Palace. The first actual raid affecting Linlithgow during class hours did not occur until 24th January 1941 and by the time the town's siren shrilled, the pupils at both the Public and Academy had been so well drilled that they carried on with their lessons in their shelters until the all clear sounded.

Despite occasional air raid warnings as German planes swept up the valley of the Forth to bomb industrial targets further to the west, Linlithgow itself was never attacked and soon was deemed a safe zone. This brought more extra work for the staffs of the local schools as they were instructed to carry out a complete survey of all homes in the town with a view to billeting evacuee children. When the first evacuees did arrive from Edinburgh in April they were housed in groups in Bonnytoun House which°stands in its wooded grounds at the east end of the loch and in Avontoun House, which has long since been demolished and Clarendon. The wee evacuees were accompanied by a teacher employed by Edinburgh Corporation Education Committee and they and she were allocated their own classroom at Linlithgow Public.

Apart from the coming of the evacuees classroom life settled back into a more or less normal school routine for the other children of the town. The dreaded 'Qualy', the qualifying examination which decided pupils' classes and type of education at the Academy was still held each May and dux medals were presented each July with summer holidays beginning on Glasgow Fair Friday, in the middle of the month.

Occasional excitements included Wings for Victory Weeks during which the boys and girls raised almost £300 including £5 from the raffle of a model bomber, as is still recorded on a plaque in the entrance hall of Old County Buildings to aid the war effort. But nothing could make up for the missing gala days or the Marches, which were kept alive by a few stalwarts but without any of the peace time pomp or pageantry. With the absence of the town's young men away fighting in the forces most sports events had also to be abandoned while the petrol shortage and the blackout, strictly imposed by the local A.R.P., made evening meetings difficult the search lights at the anti-aircraft gun establishment at Merrilees alone probing the night sky.

Linlithgow's other military presence was the establishment at Lowport of the Polish Army camp. Today the little shrine which they erected in the grounds is a lasting reminder of their faith and the wooden buildings which they occupied have been converted into Laetare International Youth Hostel where, well looked after by local District Councillor Jimmy McGinley and his wife, young visitors from many countries have the chance to make the kind of friendships which, hopefully, will make future conflict between their countries an impossibility.

On the whole the Second World War, despite the loss of the local men whose names are recorded for posterity on the town war memorial in the Queen's Aisle in St. Michael's, treated Linlithgow kindly, but it kept one of its wickedest tricks until the very last day. For it was on the morning of the day on which Victory in Europe was declared in May 1945 that a telegram was received with the news that young Robin Tudsbery of Champfleurie had been killed in action.

Robin was the only son of Sir Francis and Lady Tudsbery. Born in London the year after the end of the First World War in 1919, he came to

Champfleurie while still a baby when his family acquired the old mansion house through his mother's relations in 1921. Champfleurie, with its many historic connections with Mary Queen of Scots (who is said to have given the house its name when she exclaimed, 'C'est un vrai champ fleurie') and with Bonnie Prince Charlie who spent the night in the original house while on his triumphant progress to Edinburgh, must have been an exciting place for Robin to grow up. With his love for nature he is said to have enjoyed especially the grounds, which surround the mansion, and which had been landscaped when the house was rebuilt by Admiral Robert Hawthorn Johnston-Stewart in 1851. When he was not away at school, first at Cargilfield Preparatory School near Cramond and later at Sedbergh in Yorkshire, Robin was a familiar sight in Linlithgow to which he rode on his favourite pony.

After school Robin won a place at Kings College Cambridge. During one of the university holidays he was invited to visit India as the guest of the Viceroy, the second Marquess of Linlithgow. As soon as he graduated Robin joined the Royal Horse Guards — the Blues — and as the Second World War continued was posted overseas where he served as a lieutenant with the First Household Cavalry Regiment. On leave he was a frequent house guest at Windsor Castle, where the dashing young cavalry officer was a popular visitor with the two royal princesses. Late in 1944 he dined with them and other members of the royal family on the last night of his leave before returning to his unit in North Africa and may well have told them the news that his father, Sir Francis, who was a well known lawyer, had recently founded the Thistle Foundation for Scottish disabled servicemen.

That was Robin Tudsbery's last leave. On April 30th 1945, just as word was coming through that the war in Europe was in its closing stages, he was killed when, while on a routine patrol, the armoured vehicle which he was driving was blown up by a German land mine. The official War Office telegram announcing his death was delivered from Linlithgow post office to his parents at Champfleurie on the morning of V.E. Day.

The Robin Chapel at the Thistle Foundation at Craigmillar in Edinburgh, which was dedicated in 1953 in the presence of Queen Elizabeth, the Queen Mother, is an outstandingly beautiful and fitting memorial to him and the other Scottish servicemen who gave their lives to ensure that we could live in freedom.

That freedom was celebrated in Linlithgow as in other Scottish towns with two days of national celebrations on 8th and 9th May 1945 which were declared official holidays with all schools and businesses closed.

Shortly afterwards a General Election was called and on 28th June Mr. Churchill visited Linlithgow on his election tour. Although he was by then involved in political campaigning it was still deemed fit to close local schools early at 3.30 p.m. to enable the children to see the great war hero when he arrived at the Burgh Halls shortly after four o'clock.

A few days later a display of work and drill was presented at Linlithgow Academy on the afternoon of 3rd July. The Headteacher at the Public agreed that the two Qualifying classes should attend to show them the standard which would be expected of them when they went up to the big school after the summer holidays, but noted his displeasure in the logbook when parents asked permission for another one hundred younger pupils to attend the proceedings along at the Lowport. 'It will have to be made plain another year that there will be no release for any but those who have an immediate future interest in the Academy', declares the official entry in the log.

Official release for the first peace time summer holidays after the war came for the pupils at the Public nine days later on July 12th when Provost Ford marked the end of term by visiting the school to present the Town Council prizes to the dux boy and girl, James Anderson and Elma Gray, who had gained the highest marks in that year's Qualifying examination.

Although fighting still continued in the Pacific, there was a general feeling that the worst of the conflict was over and many Linlithgow families took the opportunity during the holidays to take their children to the seaside, which many of them had never seen before because of the war time restrictions on the coasts. It is interesting to recall that identity cards had even to be shown to get into Queensferry or Bo'ness as both lay on the Forth and were thus in a security zone, where buses and cars were all stopped and checked before entering the towns. It is also interesting to note that Linlithgow's fear of Bo'ness as a source of plague as a port town was revived as recently as the years of the last war, when smallpox broke out there in 1942. Emergency vaccination centres were set up in Linlithgow and School Medical Officer Dr. Nina Ross supervised the inoculation of all pupils, many of whom, it is noted in the school logbook, reacted so badly to the jabs that they were off ill for several days.

The enjoyment of the 1945 summer holidays was made complete by the arrival of the news on 15th August that the Japanese had at last surrendered and the Second World War was truly over. In addition to scenes of festivities on the day as local families celebrated the release from captivity of loved ones such as well known Co-operative Store manager Bobby Thomson and journalist Tom McGowran, Monday and Tuesday 15th and 16th October were officially observed throughout the whole town as V.J. Day holidays. By coincidence, Tom McGowran arrived home on Sunday 14th October after exactly three and a half years in captivity, the night before the sixth anniversary of his joining up in 1939.

Even after it had finished the war effort had to continue as the country battled on against rationing and shortages and, in the autumn of 1945, all pupils in Linlithgow were expected to go out and gather rose hips from hedgerows around the town from Bonhard to the north, to Riccarton to the south, and from Grougfoot to the east, to Lathallan to the west, to make rose hip syrup, which was supposed to be especially good for the new babies of post war Britain. Pupils at Linlithgow Public are recorded as collecting a total of 77 pounds of the rose hips which took a considerable amount of gathering as they weighed light. The newly elected Labour Government presented the school with a cheque in payment of nineteen shillings and three pence. Older pupils were also given a week off school to encourage them to go tattie howkin', but at least they were allowed to keep the money they earned from that. A special savings drive called Thanksgiving Savings Week was launched at St. Joseph's, the Public and the Academy, on 26th October and children were encouraged to take their pocket money to school every Monday morning to buy National Savings Certificates.

At the beginning of November His Majesty's Inspectors arrived to inspect all classes at Linlithgow Public. Their visit was however over in time to allow the school to hold its annual Remembrance Day Service on 9th November when all the boys and girls gathered in the assembly hall for a short act of worship which must have had a special significance that year.

One Linlithgow lady with particular memories of the Second World War years is Mrs. Cadell Snr. who was County Commissioner for the Girl Guides, Chairwoman of the Red Cross and in charge of the Women's Voluntary Service or W.V.S. At the start of the hostilities she officially handed over her Girl Guides duties to concentrate on war matters, but allowed herself to be persuaded to run a very special Brownie Pack at Bangour Hospital. This happened when the patients at East Fortune Sanatorium in East Lothian were all evacuated to make way for the R.A.F. fighter base and were rehoused at Bangour which had been declared a War Emergency Hospital. Amongst these T.B. sufferers were a whole ward full of little girls, many of them lying flat on their backs in plaster casts with T.B. spines and hips and to relieve the monotony of their years in the wards, Mrs. Cadell became their Brown Owl and confesses to using up some of her meagre W.V.S. war time petrol ration to drive across the Bathgate Hills to ensure that they enjoyed their weekly meetings for which the beds were all pulled into a circle in the middle of Ward Seven.

Back in Linlithgow, it took Mrs. Cadell longer to organise the W.V.S. to which there was, at first, a little local resistance. 'It was not that the ladies of the town did not want to help the war effort', recalls Mrs. Cadell. 'Quite the opposite! They were already so well organised through the Towns Women's Guild that they did not feel the need for another organisation. Already under the leadership of their president Mrs. Wright they had with the help of former County Clerk, Mr. J. G. B. Henderson, obtained premises in the High Street in what is now the Electricity Showroom, and opened a forces cafe. Every serviceman or woman was welcome and despite the rationing they always managed to produce home made pancakes and scones. Drivers of army convoys always knew that there would be a good hot cup of tea waiting for them in Linlithgow, and the canteen really became the centre of social life for the young people of the town. Gradually, however, as the war progressed our Lords and Masters in the government decreed that such activities should all come under the auspices of the W.V.S. and so it had to be, much to Mr. Henderson's disgust, as he was so proud of "his Linlithgow ladies" and their original local initiative.'

'The W.V.S.'s other big task was the issue of clothing to the many families in need. Wonderful parcels packed full of warm clothes arrived from Canada. We stored them in the large old house next to Miller's Garage and Mr. Scott, the lawyer, gave us the room above his office in the High Street from which to distribute them. I remember well the amount of work which the Provost's wife Mrs. Ford and her daughters, amongst others, did to sort them out and find just what each family required and I have a particular memory of young Jenny Scott, with her hair tied back in a black bow, as was the fashion of the time, delving deep into the big boxes to find shoes to fit one particular family.'

'One day a billeting officer arrived at Grange and decided that my home was big enough to take no fewer than eight evacuees. I was given a choice, not whether or not I wanted the evacuees but whether to accept boys or girls. I chose boys and they duly arrived from Edinburgh. We did have room for them in the nursery, but we simply didn't have eight beds so I burgled the Guide Hut which we still have in the grounds and found eight palliases. These I took to the farmer at Erngath and persuaded him to fill them with straw so the little boys had something to lie on for the night. Next day they started school at West Port. The townspeople were really very kind to them. At lunchtime the lady in the grocer's shop on the corner where the mini store now stands gave them cups of hot soup to keep them warm in those days before the first school meals were introduced in 1942, but they missed the city and were not very happy. As the phony war dragged on and nothing very much in the way of air raids occurred in Edinburgh several of the mothers came out to take their sons home. The boys were having a meal in the day nursery when they arrived and when one of the mothers heard that I was being paid five shillings a week to look after her boys she declared that she thought I was being paid a fortune! The remainder of the evacuees also left soon afterwards as my own children caught scarlet fever and so they were moved to join the other city youngsters at Clarendon House, where the old people's home is now.'

Chronicling events such as this week by week throughout the war was the 'Linlithgowshire Gazette's' best remembered editor, 'Paw' Brown. The ever popular 'Gazette' was founded on April 11th 1891 by F. Johnston and Company whose existing 'Falkirk Herald' had up until that time circulated widely in the western part of Linlithgowshire. Sales of the Falkirk paper were so good in Linlithgow that it was decided to launch a sister title with its headquarters in the High Street. From four pages it quickly grew to eight, but paper shortages during the First World War and the cost of what paper was available forced a reduction once again to four. During the 1920s it grew to a regular six and on occasion eight pages, packed full of detailed reports of local meetings and events. Its editor in the 1930s was Willie Raitt, whose daughter Caroline, born in Blackness is now one of Europe's most celebrated opera singers, especially in the Netherlands, where she has made her home. Then came Arthur William Brown who as the much loved 'Paw Broon' became a legend in Linlithgow. He came from the 'Dumfries Standard' and drove into town in his already veteran 1926 Alvis. In later years the old car was to become as well known as its owner, but to begin with war time petrol rationing forced 'Paw' to lay it up at Bridge House, where he also installed his wife, or 'Maw' Brown as she soon became known to the people of the 'Brig, and their young family. He first became known locally as he strode out stalking his stories on foot. One story which he did not report but which would no doubt have made the modern headlines was that as the family lived on the wrong side of the River Avon the youngest Browns Henry, Dorothy and Barbara were forbidden from going to school along the road at Linlithgow Public at West Port but were forced to go all the way to Polmont for their education.

'Paw' Brown was very much a journalist of the old school taking an interest in every local organisation and despite war time difficulties providing detailed coverage of all their activities as well as acting as war correspondent for the Johnston Group of local papers and covering the crossing of the Rhine at which he was injured. After the war when local organisations began to get back to normal it was not uncommon for him to cover as many as five meetings in one evening. Young cub reporters who were entrusted to his care received a very sound education in the art of reporting and from the familiar 'Gazette' offices in the High Street, which owners F. Johnston and Company had had specially built to house the paper in 1900, many went on to greater journalistic fame. 'Paw' Brown himself, however, was content to reign supreme over his 'Gazette', seeing it expand to take over the 'Bo'ness Journal' before he finally retired in 1967 to enjoy four years of well earned retirement before his death in 1971. His daughter, Iris, married the same Tom McGowran who had returned from the war in 1945 and subsequently became Managing Director of F. Johnston and Company and so the family's long link with local journalism lives on. His youngest daughter Barbara Braithwaite survived her enforced education in Stirlingshire to become one of Linlithgow's most faithful adopted Black Bitches and is today the only woman member of the town's Deacons' Court.

CHAPTER ELEVEN

Linlithgow Today

LINLITHGOW'S rather sleepy slow Dreamthorp existence has changed greatly since the end of the Second World War in 1945 and today it is one of the busiest small towns in Central Scotland with a population of 12,000.

Much of Linlithgow's expansion in these forty or so years has come about not so much because of events within the burgh but as a result of developments in the towns around it. First came the oil bonanza of the 1950s when the building of Scotland's only oil refinery made Grangemouth the country's 'Boom Town', as it was nicknamed, but at the same time decided many of British Petroleum's employees that they would rather live over the hill in Linlithgow's sheltered valley.

Thus began Linlithgow's new role as a dormitory town and the building of the first post war private housing estates at places such as Highfield, Friarsbrae, Clarendon and Deanburn to cater for the demand for new homes. The first folks who lived on the hill were soon joined by many other families whose fathers found that they could commute quickly and conveniently by road or rail to jobs in either Edinburgh or Glasgow.

Linlithgow's pace of progress became even faster during the 1960s when the designation of Livingston as one of Scotland's five official New Towns and the building of the giant British Motor Corporation, or B.M.C., later British Leyland, Truck and Tractor Works at Bathgate brought to the area many more families who, again, were attracted by the town's beautiful setting by the loch and by its Palace and other historic connections.

To cope with this continuously growing demand for more and more homes Priory, Oatlands, Laverock Park and Baronshill all grew up until

Coarse fishing is a popular activity in the placid waters of the Union Canal seen here where its thirty five foot width broadens in the Manse Basin, which was once Linlithgow's busy inland harbour and is now the scene of the headquarters for Linlithgow Union Canal Society and Linlithgow Canoe Club. Several of LUCS's craft can be seen including one of its cabin cruises and lying alongside the quay the replica 19th century steam paquet 'Victoria', which provides cruises for school groups and members of the public throughout the summer season.

only their place names remained as a reminder of the farms which once flourished and the skylarks which formerly nested on these lands. Where once townsfolk had enjoyed quiet Sunday afternoon country walks more and more built up areas appeared as estate after estate such as Belsyde, Longcroft, Lennox Gardens and Avontoun were each in turn sold to the developers. Avontoun is particularly interesting because before building houses, a quarry was opened to supply foundation material for the M9 motorway and in 1969 was filled in with rubble from the demolition work in the High Street. The Avontoun Park houses had subsequently to be built on rafts of concrete to provide suitable foundations.

Largest expansion of all took place to the east of the town first at sprawling Springfield, whose sheer size is best seen from the railway line to Edinburgh, and latterly at Blackness Road. Linlithgow now stretches almost to the M9 motorway at Champany, la campagne of Mary Queen of Scots' royal picnickers.

Linlithgow is still expanding with ever more private housing developments at Riccarton, Carmelaws, Beechwood, Mains Maltings and Kettilstoun. At Kettilstoun, about the spelling of which arguments exist, guarantees have been given that there will be adequate provision for sports fields and recreational areas and it can only be regretted that similar provision has not been made in many of the earlier developments.

This lack of community provision is seen at its worst in Springfield. Virtually large enough to be a small new town in its own right it has only a primary school with a small community wing and not a single shop although four are now planned. While the countryside around Linlithgow was built up, sadly, many of the old buildings right at the very heart of the town at the Cross and west along the northside of the High Street were demolished. Amongst the historic buildings swept away were the Golden Cross Cafe, the Cunzie Neuk pub and the Spanish Ambassador's House with its finely crafted plaster ceilings, along with several of the town houses used by the nobles when they dwelt in Linlithgow to be close to the royal court.

The blame for this act of official vandalism, which has since been bitterly regretted, lay with the members of Linlithgow Town Council who stubbornly refused to heed a national campaign led by well known Scottish actor Moultrie Kelso to consider alternative plans to save the old town. It was true that some of the High Street tenements had been allowed to deteriorate and were in need of repair. It was also true that some of them were Victorian, less than a hundred years old and in any other setting perhaps than Linlithgow High Street of little real historic interest. What the town councillors of Linlithgow in the 1960s totally failed to appreciate in their desire to create new council housing, was that their High Street was a very special treasure amongst Scottish domestic architecture which needed equally special thought and treatment if the whole was not to be irreparably ruined by the destruction of its parts.

Today twenty years later in the 1980s the demolition of the High Street would not even be contemplated but in the 1960s ideas about conservation were not so developed and the Linlithgow councillors failed to grasp that good solidly constructed buildings of stone and slate could be sympathetically modernised to provide decades more of excellent accommodation. It is indeed a pity that the Linlithgow councillors had not been better advised by their officials and, in particular, that no-one suggested that they leave their chamber in the Town House and, like the merchants in past centuries, sail across the North Sea to the Netherlands where they could have seen preservation techniques such as saving the facades of historic streets while building modern apartments behind the old frontages.

As if they had not sinned enough the former Linlithgow councillors went on to commit their gravest sin of all when the demolition was complete. For then instead of at least leaving the north side of the High Street open to allow what could have been magnificent views across the loch, they chose to erect some of the ugliest modern flat roofed accommodation ever built in any Scottish town. To the horror of the townsfolk these three and four storey monstrosities were built from the Vennel to West Port. Officially, they incorporated traditional Scottish features such as harling on the walls and imitation concrete cobbles on the pavement outside, with the most modern of Scottish 1960s architecture and the so-called experts duly sung their praises in true Hans Christian Andersen 'King's New Clothes' fashion. 'The entire scheme is a notable example of bold and imaginative thinking, and both the town authority and the architects have rightly earned a great deal of praise for this project', declared 'The Scotsman' of Tuesday September 9th 1969, while the Saltire Society presented the dreadful development with a special award. Only the local people, like the wee boy in the fairy tale, protested from those who had to live in the damp, leaking, crumbling flat topped abominations, to those whose eyes were insulted by them every time they walked along the High Street and remembered all that had been swept away and sacrificed in the name of progress.

The Linlithgow flats became a national joke especially when the architects compounded their folly by persuading the Town Council to allow them to squander several thousand extra pounds on building Scotland's most unusual bus shelter. This strange fan shaped edifice was duly built on the south side of the High Street at its junction with Preston Road where the experts assured the Councillors that it provided a perfect balance with the West Port flats on the opposite side. As soon as it was built it became apparent that it was so badly designed that it did not provide bus passengers with any form of shelter, but that it did effectively prevent them from seeing the buses. In the end after years of protests from local residents Linlithgow's West Port folly was demolished.

Now in the six hundredth centenary year the problem of the High Street flats is at last also being tackled under an imaginative renovation scheme thought up by the architects department of Lothian District Council with the encouragement of both of the town's current representatives on the Council, Councillor James Clark and Councillor Jimmy McGinley. Under this scheme the appearance of the flats is being transformed by the addition of traditionally Scottish looking pitched roofs clad in slate and red pantiles, while the harling problems which have marred large areas of the flats for years are being tackled by the application of carefully chosen colour washes again in the tradition of Scottish domestic architecture. At the same time other decorative features on the flats, which were out of keeping with their setting in the High Street of a historic Scottish town, such as the extensive use of wood around the window areas, are being removed. The end result should be that the flats should fit in much more harmoniously with their surroundings than they have ever done before, while at the same time providing much more comfortable living conditions for the families who occupy them by the elimination of damp.

At the same time another of the buildings erected as a major feature of the High Street redevelopment, Peel House, is also being given a new lease of life. Built originally in 1969 as a supermarket and small department store by Bo'ness Co-operative Society in an ambitious but unsuccessful attempt to keep up with the latest trends in shopping patterns, Peel House is currently being converted into the local health centre, which Linlithgow has long required. When the work is completed the present small health clinic in the Vennel will be freed for other community uses, a move which will again be welcome in the town, where such facilities have never been sufficient.

Sadly the failure of Peel House as a shopping centre to attract sufficient customers brought to an end the history of the Co-operative Movement in the town which started in 1925 as after the local society merged with Scotmid in 1982 it was decided in 1984 that there was no longer sufficient support to continue operating in the town. Thus Linlithgow was left as one of the few places in Scotland without its 'Store'.

While the Co-operative Movement failed in Linlithgow, other organisations have flourished. They include the Civic Trust, the Arts Guild, the History and Amenity Society whose local history library is now housed within the modern public library in the Vennel, the Black Bitch Association, the Rotary Club, the Round Table, the Forty One Club, Link, Linlithgow Lore, Lamp (Linlithgow Amateur Musical Productions), The Linlithgow Players' Drama Club, the Horticultural Society and, even, a Leek Club. Sports clubs include athletics, badminton, bowls, cricket, canoeing, football, golf, martial arts, orienteering, rugby, sailing, and tennis and squash, taken together with the many flourishing church and youth organisations such as Boy Scouts, Girl Guides, Boys Brigade and Linlithgow Bridge Majorettes, the list and variety seems almost endless.

The main problem for most of these organisations in the town is, undoubtedly, finding suitable accommodation for their meetings and activities. This has been helped slightly by the recent completion of St. Michael's fine new church hall designed by William Cadell, Architects, which will complement their existing Church House. But Linlithgow still lacks the large community centre it so much needs.

The nearest which the town has come to community provision is the recent completion of the fine new Lowport Centre. Built by Lothian Region it will exploit the many opportunities for outdoor sporting pursuits available on Linlithgow Loch and in the surrounding Bathgate Hills and will certainly attract many visitors to the town, but its indoor facilities for use by local people are much more limited than had been hoped for and a public swimming pool is still much missed. The fact that the new centre at Lowport offers residential accommodation for thirty eight visitors will give a particularly welcome boost to Linlithgow's tourism potential. This is particularly important for while the town has welcomed the highly sophisticated Racal defence equipment factory to Riccarton and looks forward to the building of the new American Sun Microsystems computer factory at Burgh Muir, tourism is now its largest and fastest growing industry.

Since the late Father McGovern of St. Michael's R.C. Church had the foresight way back in the war years to found Laetare International Youth Hostel first in a cottage on the shores of the Loch and later after peace returned in the buildings previously used to house the Free Polish forces at Lowport, more and more visitors have been coming to discover the many delights which Linlithgow has to offer.

While Linlithgow's magnet to attract tourists will always be its links with Mary Queen of Scots, the Palace and St. Michael's are now far from the only places of interest to visitors. Two history trails, laid out by Academy history teacher Bruce Jamieson and his pupils, are sign posted throughout the town taking in not only the High Street but also the very attractive Victorian conservation area of substantial stone built villas and terraces between the railway and the canal which has its own particularly peaceful charm. Royal Terrace, Strawberry Bank, Union Road and Friars Brae all have features worth discovering and make a rewarding stroll.

The canal itself offers in addition to Scotland's only canal museum, cruises on the *Victoria*, boats for hire and towpath walks all the way out

West Lothian's only circular beehived shaped stone built doocot stands on the town side of Manse Basin in Learmonth Gardens from whose vantage point the golden crown of thorns on top of St. Michael's stone steeple can also be seen. The ground where the doocot stands was originally the tail end of the run rig belonging to Baron Ross of Halkhead. Only the nobles and landed gentry were allowed to own doocots as the birds ate large quantities of grain while waiting to be fattened for the pies which added welcome variety to their rich owners' winter diets, while poorer inhabitants had to exist on rank salt beef slaughtered months earlier in the autumn because of lack of winter fodder before the coming of root vegetables such as turnips. The pigeon holes by which the birds gained entry through the three foot thick walls to the almost 400 nesting boxes inside can be seen as can the stone ropes or ridges which thwarted any rats or other vermin from climbing up to attack them.

to the Avon Aqueduct. That walk leads on to Muiravonside Country Park with its wooded walks, its attractive farm steading visitor centre and its painstakingly restored doocot.

Muiravonside's doocot is a reminder of the days when only lairds were allowed to keep much prized pigeons not to race but to put in their pies during the winter months, when lack of winter fodder such as root vegetables meant a dearth of fresh beef, pork or mutton. The doocot is of a traditional stone built rectangular design, and faces south, so that when the doos came out of their pigeon holes on the same side they could enjoy the sun beating down on the steeply raked slate roof. It was not only the comfort of the birds that the laird was concerned about but also their safety for he had no wish to see them eaten until he was ready for them. This meant that the doocot had to be constructed to prevent the pigeons falling prey to foxes, rodents or human poachers. To keep out the animal predators a stone rope or course was constructed right round the whole of the doocot so that their attempts to climb up and in the pigeon holes were always thwarted. The human poachers were equally effectively kept out by installing double locked doors, the inner one made of iron.

Linlithgow's other doocot can also be seen easily by visitors as it is situated right on the banks of the Union Canal at Manse Basin. It is of a much more unusual circular design, but like the one at Muiravonside its inner walls are again ringed with hundreds of nesting boxes. They stretch right up to the stone ceiling but when it was time for the pot or the pie there was no hiding place for the plump young pigeons as a ladder attached to a pole in the centre of the doocot allowed them all to be reached. Another small doocot can also still be seen high in the eaves of the attic of Hamilton's Land at the east end of the High Street.

Birdwatching of a much less violent kind is now another of Linlithgow's tourist attractions down at the sanctuary at the east end of the Loch. Although it is interesting all year round it is best visited in winter when it plays host to large numbers of migrating geese, all carefully watched over by bird watching enthusiasts whose shared interest spans the generations from Lt. Col. Ponsonby and his wife to young Rebecca Helliwell, who has already featured on several television programmes about her beloved swans.

The bird sanctuary is the only interruption to the path which provides a walk right round the loch, popular with both residents and visitors alike. The area around Linlithgow offers walkers many other pleasant strolls including well marked footpaths in the Bathgate Hills, where information can be obtained about them from the unusual Scandinavian style turf roofed visitor centre at Whitebaulks in the middle of Beecraigs Country Park.

For those who want to do something more energetic than simply walk or jog, Beecraigs' seven hundred acres offers a wide range of sports.

These include dinghy sailing, kayak canoeing, open Canadian canoeing, rock climbing, mountain biking, orienteering, pioneering which involves problem solving, and target archery, but it is for field archery that it is particularly famous.

Field archery involves participants walking round a course somewhat similar to a golf course firing at animal shaped targets set at varying distances. Beecraigs has the best field archery course in Britain and has already hosted the European Field Archery Competition.

Strictly not for shooting are Beecraigs' red deer, one of Scotland's finest herds. Beecraigs Loch which was originally excavated as a water supply reservoir by German prisoners during the First World War from 1914 to 1918, provides excellent fishing for trout and the park also has its own fish farm, the only one owned by a local authority in Britain.

Venison and trout from Beecraigs now feature on many local restaurant menus just as these delicacies used to do at Palace feasts. Medieval banquets, held within the Palace, are now organised once again each August as yet another tourist attraction. The banquets are always one of the highlights of the Linlithgow Festival Week, which is the only local celebration in Scotland with an official link with the Edinburgh Festival.

Over the years the Linlithgow festival's attractions have ranged from son et lumiere in St. Michael's to Middle Ages style jousting on the Peel and from recreations of pitched 'battles' between Roundheads and Cavaliers to a play about Ninian Winzet by local author Tom McGowran.

Unique to the Palace are its junior guides, another Linlithgow tourism project. The junior guides whose ages range from 10 to 14 started eight years ago as a distinctly different history project at Linlithgow Primary School. So popular did they prove with visitors that Palace custodian Ian Ballantyne encouraged them to stay on and provide tours at weekends and during holidays. Since then, the young guides have gained fame through many television and radio appearances and now make their own costumes and write their own music to entertain the many visitors whom they enjoy welcoming to Linlithgow each year.

The young guides now also help at St. Michael's Church and at Hopetoun House and the pride which they take in introducing tourists to the history of their town and its surrounding district augurs well for the future of Linlithgow.

For while Linlithgow has a long and rich past to celebrate in this the six hundredth anniversary year of its achieving the proud status of being a Royal Burgh, it is to its young people that it must look to carry on its traditions into the future.

During the early 1980's Scottish Television provided a wider audience for the pupils of Linlithgow Primary School by broadcasting several events from the school. These included a Christmas party, excerpts from the school's production of 'Wizard of Oz' and a Burns Supper, seen here, with 11 year old David Grant as chairman of the proceedings. The Immortal Memory was proposed by Elizabeth Bowman, the Selkirk Grace was said by little Siobhan Harvey, the toast to the Lassies was proposed by Neil Mowat and replied to by Janet Smyth and 'Tam O'Shanter' was recited by Jacqueline Cummings and illustrated by an animated cartoon drawn by other pupils at the school.

Judging from the enthusiasm which they show each June for the town's famous Riding of the Marches, these traditions are in safe hands. For no matter whether residents are true Black Bitches, born and bred in the town, or the latest newcomers, the First Tuesday after the Second Thursday in June is still undoubtedly Linlithgow's big day.

The excitement actually begins on the previous Friday with the ancient tradition of the Crying of the Marches. As in olden days a fine could be levied on any of the inhabitants who did not attend the Marches, it was obviously very important that all of the townsfolk be reminded of the forthcoming event. This was always done by the Town Crier and nowadays Linlithgow is the only town in Scotland with an official crier. Once upon a time Linlithgow's Town Crier would have announced every event from news of price increases at the market at the Cross to funerals, but now his duties are mainly connected with the Marches, starting with the crying at one o'clock on the preceding Friday afternoon.

As tradition demands the first crying takes place on the spot where the Whitten Fountain used to stand in the middle of the road at the start of the High Street at Lowport and from there crier John Watson, as his predecessors have always done, stops at regular intervals the entire length of the street until he finally reaches West Port. At each halt, and introduced by 'tuck of drums' as it always used to be described he shouts, 'Oh Yez, Oh Yez, Oh Yez. The burgesses, craftsmen and whole inhabitants of Linlithgow are hearby warned and summoned to attend my Lord Provost, Bailies and Council at the ringing of the bells on Tuesday for the purpose of riding the Town's Marches and liberties according to the use and custom of the ancient and honorable Burgh and that in their best carriage, equipage, apparel and array and also to attend all diets of court held and appointed on that day by my Lord Provost and Bailies and that under the penalty of One Hundred Pounds Scotch each. God save the Queen and My Lord Provost.'

The Crier always wears his distinctive black velvet suit with plumed bonnet and as well as the drummers is always accompanied by his guard, the halberdiers with their tall top hats and long shafted axe like picks. This quaint entourage is in turn accompanied by all of the town's school children right along the flag bedecked High Street past all of the freshly painted shop fronts and in the past newly whitewashed closes to the final crying which used to take place at West Port, but which now for safety reasons is performed within the playground of Linlithgow Primary's original Public School buildings, where young brass players from all of the town's primary schools play for the crowds as they await the appearance of the Crier over the brow of the brae at West Port.

One bairn who recalled these annual Friday escapes from the classroom was Black Bitch David Morrison who, when exiled in New York, wrote a letter home which vividly captured these childhood memories. 'I see myself again as a Burgh School pupil', he wrote, 'longing for the Friday preceding the great event, when the town herald, Jock the Blackie, attired in his new velvet suit with red stockings and buckled shoes and cocked bonnet with feather, gathered us all around him for the Crying. Like a great orchestra leader he would direct and time us with his drum stick in the opening 'O Yez, O Yez, O Yez' of his proclamation. Again I

Headmaster of Linlithgow Primary School and author of this book, William F. Hendrie, is seen receiving the Scotsman Trophy for the best primary or secondary school newspaper produced in Scotland, an honour which the school has won five times including four years in a row in 1985, '86, '87 and '88.

am keeping step to 'Roke', played by flautist Muir and drummer Bowie as I find myself marching along the High Street with my school mates. I leave the crowd at the Cross and return to the Burgh School, realising that if I were late 'Baldie' or 'Bull Dog' Walker or 'Coal Jack' Forrester would greet me with the tawse.'

With Linlithgow's great leather making tradition it is interesting to wonder if that thick, thonged tawse was made right here in Linlithgow by old Gillespie the saddler. Nowadays, the children are given an extended lunch hour to encourage them to keep up the old traditions.

Marches Day itself starts early with the drums and flutes out at crack of dawn playing at the homes of local dignitaries. Traditionally this dawn start was dictated by the fact that the Provost and his officials had to be up at dawn in order to give them time to audit the town's financial affairs so that they could certify that the books were all in good order at the Provost's Breakfast. Today it is putting last minute touches to the wonderfully imaginative decorated floats and tableaux for the Marches procession which requires many people to be up at dawn and indeed it is doubtful if many Marches enthusiasts even bother to go to bed so great is the excitement before the big event.

Today all the work of organising the Marches is carried out by the members of the Deacon's Court and an invitation to the Provost's Breakfast in the Burgh Halls is still considered a great honour.

Bacon and eggs and freshly baked morning rolls have now replaced the salt herring eaten to encourage a drouth in years gone by, but the speeches and toasts even at this early hour of the morning always remain as witty and as pointed as ever. The breakfast, in the crowded Lower Hall, is also always a time to remember exiled Black Bitches around the world.

Amongst those always in attendance at the breakfast are all of the Deacons and My Lords of the various organisations, who have been installed on the previous two Saturday evenings on the steps of the Town House.

After the breakfast they, and the other guests including civic leaders from other neighbouring towns with local traditions such as Lanark, Queensferry and even Bo'ness join the Provost in his magnificent ermine trimmed robe to march up the Kirk Gate to the forecourt of the Palace. Here they all form two long lines to greet, shake hands and wish 'Happy Marches' to all of the members of other organisations such as the top hatted Dyers and the deer stalker sporting '41 Clubbers', who climb the hill to join them. This is called fraternising.

Together they then make their way back down to the Cross, where the results of the various Marches competitions, including those for decorated floats and tableaux are announced from the steps of the Town House.

Shortly before eleven o'clock the fencing of the court then takes place with the Town Clerk reading and the Town Crier John Watson announcing the following proclamation.

'I defend and I forbid in our Sovereign Lady's name, and in name of My Lord Provost, and Bailies of the Royal Burgh of Linlithgow, that no person or persons presume nor take upon hand, under whatever colour or pretext to trouble or molest the Magistrates and Burgesses in their peaceful riding of the town's Marches under all highest pains and charges that after may follow. God save the Queen.'

The actual Riding then begins with the marshalling of the procession, ready to drive off westward along the flag bedecked, crowd packed High Street exactly on the stroke of eleven o'clock.

The courtyard at Linlithgow Palace always makes a dignified setting for the formal pictures taken on gala days in July. The Linlithgow and Linlithgow Bridge Gala was started in 1920 and since 1930 the main event of the day has been the crowning of a school girl queen. On this occasion in 1968 the young queen was Margaret Kilbride and she is seen accompanied by her girl train bearers and her boy crown and sceptre bearers. The adults in the picture included from left to right Mrs. Margaret Glen, Police Judge Sandy Merker, Mrs. Merker, Mrs. Daisy Marshall, Bailie Robert Marshall, Mrs. Byrne, Provost Byrne, Mrs. Reid, Bailie David Cook, Councillor Mrs. Julia Wade, Mr. Stephen Haluch, Councillor Mrs. Betty Haluch, Mrs. Bain and Councillor Peter Bain, who was President of the Gala Committee. Above on the fountain can be seen figures of 16th century Linlithgow worthies preserved for posterity in stone when the mason carved them during the reign of King James V. They include the town drummer, a merchant of the burgh and a priest.

There are now, sadly, far fewer horses in the Marches procession but the Provost and Magistrates do still ride in open horse drawn landau. As well as more horses processions of former years also used to feature the banners of the trade guilds. As well as their own distinctive flags each guild also delighted in making its decorated float reflect its craft by including tools of its trade and examples of the goods which its members produced throughout the year. This meant for instance that the Hammermen's decorated cart bore a large hammer and anvil, while the Wright's pony trap, which was decorated all over with curly wood shavings, carried a small bench at which worked the cut out figures of two joiners, whose arms sawed away, powered by elastic bands, pulled in turn by the youngest apprentice.

Slogans were also very popular on the craft guild floats the leather working Cordiners boasting, 'Our trade is ever lasting' and 'True to the Last', while the baxters asked, 'Can man live by bread alone? Yes, if it's baked by Oliphants!'

As the procession makes its excited way westward all of the town's bells ring out and continue ringing until it passes the Horse Market Head beyond the West Port.

While the crowds which line the High Street and, especially those who gather at West Port, are always enthusiastic, it is said that the people of Linlithgow Bridge are never outdone in the reception which they give the procession when it arrives at the Bridge Inn. Here at the old whitewashed inn the Waldie Loving Cup, donated by Alexander Spence the Deacon of the Dyers in 1922, is always ready filled to the brim to provide welcome refreshment.

The nearby bridge across the River Avon is the most westerly of Linlithgow's marches or bounds and after various toasts, to 'The Marches' and 'The People of the Brig' are drunk, the procession moves off again, eastward, this time back towards Linlithgow. As soon as it re-appears at West Port, its return is spotted by the lookout at the top of the Town House clock tower, who gives the signal for the bells to peal out again to announce its safe return.

According to F. C. Eele writing in 'Church Bells of Linlithgowshire', published in 1912, the bells then continue, 'while the procession passes eastwards on the way to Blackness. As it passes out of sight at the Duke's Entry, the ringing ceases.' (While as an outsider Mr. Eele spells it Duke's entry most Black Bitches deny this regal connection and insist that it is the Duicks' Entry where the ducks have always waddled their way down to the Loch!)

Traditionally it was considered a great honour to be the first carriage into the Square at Blackness, but on the last lap into the village many carriages do, equally traditionally, make an unscheduled halt at the top of the brae leading down into the old seaport at what is reliably reported to be the best watered and fastest growing hedge in Scotland.

At Blackness all of the participants are formally welcomed by the

'Happy Marches', the well chosen title of this lively mural, by American artist Mary Couloris, who is now resident in Linlithgow, well captures the boisterous enjoyment of the famous local saying and the day each June when it is the standard greeting amongst all Black Bitches and others who are lucky enough to share in their annual festivities. The colourful mural, which greets passengers at Linlithgow Railway Station and which was commissioned to mark the re-opening of the modernised station depicts the many Marches celebrations against a background of well known Linlithgow landmarks from the Kirk Gate on the left to the offices on the right from which the 'The Linlithgowshire Journal and Gazette' is published every week.

Baron Bailie. The present Baron Bailie is village postmaster Robert Fleming and although, unlike his predecessors, he can no longer fine smugglers or flog wrong doers, he still reports each Marches Day on the safe conduct of village affairs during the preceding year. Toasts are then drunk in Blackness Milk, liberally laced with whisky, to give all present renewed energy to climb Castle Hill for the fencing of the court on the site of St. Ninian's Chapel.

After a leisurely lunch with many toasts and equally many drinks the participants then make their way back to Lowport ready for the climax to the whole day when at 5 o'clock the bells ring out again and the procession, supplemented by many of the local inhabitants parades back along the High Street.

It then makes its way a traditional three times round the Cross Well, which is said to be a direct link with pagan times when three was considered a lucky number. When the procession has completed its third round, which was always traditionally made at a particularly fast pace, My Lord Provost and the Deacons all drink each others healths on the steps of the Town House and bid each other 'Safe oot, safe in' and the proceedings then officially end with the whole crowd joining in the singing of 'Auld Lang Syne'.

Celebrations and festivities, however, always continue on well into the night whether in the pubs or at the 'shows' and the fact that the following day is a Recovery Day holiday is still as welcome as ever.

In 1989 the Marches will only mark the start of a whole summer of celebrations organised by a committee led by Provost Baird. The highlight of these festivities will be a visit by Her Majesty the Queen on Friday, 7th July and the festivities will continue right through until Saturday 21st October when Her Majesty's predecessor King Robert II's granting of the charter creating Linlithgow a Royal Burgh will be suitably re-enacted. As night falls both the Palace and St. Michael's will share the limelight as the new floodlights donated by 'The Linlithgowshire Journal and Gazette' to mark this six hundredth anniversary year are switched on and the townsfolk, the loyal lieges of Linlithgow march in torchlit procession through the old streets to the Peel to watch as the fireworks blaze and are reflected in the loch, the loch which has flowed through all of 'Lithgow's' long and illustrious life.

Bibliography

History of Linlithgow Palace   Dr. John Ferguson
History of St. Michael's Church   Dr. John Ferguson
The Rocks of West Lothian   Henry M. Cadell
The Story of the Forth   Henry M. Cadell
A History of the Town and Place of Linlithgow   George Waldie
Walks Along the Northern Roman Wall   George Waldie
Linlithgow at the Scottish Reformation and in the 17th Century   James
   Beveridge
Linlithgowshire Past and Present   Archibald C. M'Michael
Place Names of West Lothian   M. Johnston
Linlithgowshire   Cambridge County Geographies
Church Bells of Linlithgowshire   F. C. Eele
First Statistical Account
Second Statistical Account

The above books are all out of print but copies of most may be consulted at West Lothian County History and Amenity Society's library, which is housed within Linlithgow Public Library at the Vennel. Membership of the History Society carries with it the privilege of borrowing books from its very comprehensive collection and of attendance at its meetings which are held on the evenings of the third Wednesday of each month in the autumn, spring and winter with the exception of December and January. Summer outings are also organised. Full details may be obtained from the Hon. Secretary, Mrs Ann Crichton, Old Farmhouse, Niddry Mains, Winchburgh.

West Lothian History Society also publishes booklets including,

Sudden Slaughter, The Murder of the Regent Moray   Patrick Cadell
Sanctuary and the Privilege of St. John   P. H. R. Mackay
West Lothian Miscellany

Other books on Linlithgow and district currently available in print include,

Linlithgow in Old Picture Postcards   Bruce Jamieson
Bathgate and Torphichen in Old Picture Postcards   William F. Hendrie
Bo'ness in Old Picture Postcards   William F. Hendrie
all published by the European Library, Zaltbommel, Netherlands.
Discovering West Lothian   William F. Hendrie published by John Donald, Edinburgh.
The Morn's The Fair, A History of West Lothian folk celebrations including Linlithgow Marches   William F. Hendrie published by the author and available from 'The Old School House' Torphichen.
Linlithgow Heritage Trails, two illustrated leaflets compiled by Bruce Jamieson and available from the Tourist Information Centre, Forth Valley Tourist Board, Burgh Halls, Linlithgow, which also has a full supply of coloured illustrated leaflets on Linlithgow, Beecraigs Country Park and other West Lothian places of interest published by West Lothian District Council Public Relations Section for the Department of Leisure and Recreation, Old County Buildings, Linlithgow.
The latest edition of the Linlithgow Town Guide was published by the Community Council in 1988 and contains full details of all local services and businesses.
For even more up to date information 'The Linlithgowshire Journal and Gazette' is published every Friday and is available from its offices in the High Street and all local newsagents.
'The Lothian Courier', published weekly in Bathgate also covers the Linlithgow district.

Index